Mrs. Frances Laurence
850 Webster St. Apt. 1000
Palo Alto, CA 94301

MARY LOU

This fetching little creature, made from the simplest pattern for a soft rag doll, has the charm and personality of a real little girl. Her blonde hair is knitting yarn, and her features are delicately embroidered on, with freckles to give a touch of piquancy.

The Complete Book of

Doll Making and Collecting

BY

CATHERINE CHRISTOPHER

SECOND REVISED EDITION

DOVER PUBLICATIONS, INC.
NEW YORK

This Dover edition, first published in 1971, is
a revised republication of the work originally published by The Greystone Press, New York, in
1949. A new Preface has been written for the
present edition by the author.

Standard Book Number: 486-22066-4
Library of Congress Catalog Card Number: 76-102176

Manufactured in the United States of America
Dover Publications, Inc.
180 Varick Street
New York, N.Y. 10014

Preface to the Dover Edition

THE INTEREST IN DOLL MAKING AND DOLL COLLECTING THAT has developed during the past twenty years is phenomenal. Doll clubs now exist all over the country, doll shows are presented regularly and a good many small museums devoted to toys and dolls have been established by historical societies, private endowments and individual communities. State and local craftsmen's guilds and their outlet shops as well as thousands of gift shops include handmade dolls in their shows and on their shelves. Several public school systems, notably those of Detroit, Michigan, and Brooklyn, N.Y., maintain children's museums in which important segments of the collections are dolls that are used in traveling exhibits to the schools as well as in displays in the museums.

Concurrently, the enormous increase in interest in the needle arts of embroidery and dressmaking has developed skills that are very important to the doll maker. When applied in miniature to dolls they become fixed for the future, a permanent and cherished example of artistry and expert needlework.

Discard the idea that a so-called rag doll is a play doll for a child. The truth of the matter is that it isn't! The average modern child much prefers a highly realistic commercially made plastic doll with all its highly realistic costumes and accessories. The appeal of the doll you design, make and dress will be primarily adult. It is in essence a showcase for your skills and more often than not will become the nucleus of a collection. No matter what its ultimate role will be, do write your name and date of making on its torso with India ink. Such data are invaluable to a future owner.

Right now doll collecting has more devotees than was dreamed possible some years ago. To acquire an 18th century doll today you would need a stroke of extraordinary luck and/or a limitless checkbook. Those in existence are either already in museums or in important private collections slated for museums. The 19th century doll continues to turn up in shops, auctions, antique

7

shows, in advertisements and through private dickering. Prices have quadrupled since the late 1940's.

Many dolls made between 1900 and 1940 are highly desirable. The really good ones are quite as scarce and as expensive as good antique ones. This is where membership in an accredited doll club pays off. Through its activities and programs you learn selectivity, values and possible sources of supply. The production of commercial dolls during the mid-20th century is incalculable and highly confusing to the novice collector. As a doll maker it is relatively easy to assess the value and interest of other handmade dolls. The commercially made one is something else again. It is to your advantage to acquire know-how from experienced collectors.

Buying foreign dolls at their point of origin is an idea that many American travelers put high up on their shopping lists. Every foreign airport, railroad station and near-by tourist trap has dolls for sale. Most of them are better left right there since they are cheap (in taste) and gaudy little travesties designed to catch the tourist dollar. Because the American interest in dolls is well known abroad you'll find really good dolls in shops some distance from the terminals. Be prepared to pay prices equivalent to those in the United States.

Either to the maker or the collector, or both, dolls provide avenues of unending interest. Even the most cursory study of their backgrounds, costumes and manufacture brings into focus a fascinating world you might otherwise have missed. Welcome to it!

Flemington, New Jersey
October, 1969

Dolls and You

THE FASCINATION OF DOLLS BECOMES APPARENT ONLY WHEN one has really looked at them from a point of view other than that embodied in the thought of "Oh, I guess I'll get Mary another doll for her birthday!" You vaguely remember that no little girl ever had too many dolls. Each one was endowed with a personality all its own. That is no less true today, even if you are grown up and interested in more serious things. The difference between today and yesterday lies only in the loss of childhood magic which allowed imaginations to run riotously through far places and fanciful scenes.

However, as this book will show you, dolls can still work that magic for you. They can take you into the far corners of the world and reveal an absorbing cross section of the historic and social past. They can open the gate that will allow your creative impulses to develop into real skills.

The urge to do something with one's hands, to make something lovely and individual, is perfectly expressed in making dolls. One of our aims here is to help you realize that urge easily and pleasantly. Simple as your first efforts may be, the evolution of a distinct doll personality under your unaccustomed fingers is immediately evident. You may start off with nothing more concrete in mind than just to make a doll. Yet the doll emerges, perhaps not with beauty, but with an individuality and character all its own. Try it and see. So strong is this doll magic that making three or four of the dolls in this book is just a beginning. Before long you will have become a confirmed doll maker—and you will find a whole gallery of lovely dolls, from the simple to the elaborate, for you to choose from in the following pages. You will have a hobby, delightful in itself, and one that contains the possibility of becoming a modestly profitable enterprise. Suggestions are given in a later chapter for capitalizing on your hobby.

Your own dolls, of course, will be a continual source of interest and pleasure to you. But it is inevitable that your interest will widen to embrace the whole field of dolls, and much of this book is planned to satisfy that interest. Antique dolls, dolls of other nations, character dolls of the past and present, story-book and folk dolls will all exert their gentle and subtle influence. They, too, were made as creative expressions, but over and above the fact lies the absorbing story each doll represents. Discovering those stories lifts the curtain on the past, gives you personal and intimate glimpses of history that were never contained in your school books. Consider these fascinating facts, for example:

Did you know that at one time dolls were considered so important that ships carrying them were accorded neutrality between nations at war?

Did you know that once, during the Civil War, precious medicines and drugs were smuggled through to the Confederate soldiers by being carried inside a doll's head?

Did you know that many public schools in the United States use real dolls with which to teach history, sociology, arts and crafts, as well as in studies to eradicate racial prejudice and develop appreciation of other peoples and other lands?

Did you know that there are over two hundred and twenty-five million dolls in this country, and that the majority of them are owned by adults?

The fact remains, that, while mute, the doll is highly expressive of a variety of significant factors. More enduring than some of the mightiest monuments ever built, the doll has persisted throughout the ages as an imperishable expression of men's dreams. Unwittingly the doll reveals the tremendous scope of man's endeavors, inventive ingenuity, manufacturing zeal. The doll has portrayed political whims, even national bloodthirstiness, as did the wooden doll which was made during the latter part of the nineteenth century in Vermont expressly for export to Japan. This doll had an ingenious arrangement which allowed the Japanese child to decapitate the doll without destroying it!

Above any other fascinations which the doll holds for us—as you will discover when you make any of the dozens of lovely dolls in this book—is the fact that it is the successful expression of creative effort designed to delight both its maker and its subsequent owner.

CATHERINE CHRISTOPHER

Contents

Acknowledgments

THE AUTHOR WISHES TO EXPRESS GRATITUDE AND APPRECIA-
tion to the many people who have directly and indirectly
helped her in obtaining material for this book. Their time and
energy were given with generosity and enthusiasm which added in
no small measure to the pleasure of completing such a work.

Special thanks are due the following for their unstinting co-
operation, information and advice: Mrs. Edward B. Cole, Doll
Museum, Wenham, Mass.; Miss Gertrude Townsend, Museum
of Fine Arts, Boston, Mass.; Mrs. A. E. MacSwiggan, Essex Institute, Salem, Mass.; Miss Margaret M. Brayton, Children's Museum, Detroit, Mich.; Mrs. Ralph Sandt, Sandt Doll Hospital,
Easton, Pa.

For the loan of dolls for photographic purposes and for making
special photographs available for use in this book, the author
thanks those friends and owners.

Historic societies, museums and other agencies and persons have
also made invaluable contributions, particularly the Metropolitan
Museum of Art, New York City; Bostonian Society, Boston,
Mass.; Independence Hall, Philadelphia, Pa.; Pennsylvania His-
torical Society, Philadelphia, Pa.; the Shelburne Museum,
Shelburne, Vt.; the Smithsonian Institution, Washington,
D. C.; the Brooklyn Children's Museum, Brooklyn, N. Y.

1.

Soft Rag Dolls Are Easy To Make

*A*S COMPLETELY AMERICAN AS MAPLE SYRUP AND PAN-cakes, the rag doll can be made by anyone capable of running up a seam either by hand or on the machine. There are few limits to the possibilities inherent in the rag doll. It can be as simple and charming or as elaborate and beautiful as you wish to make it. You can use old scraps just as effectively and imaginatively as any special material purchased expressly for this purpose.

As well as being a lot of fun, doll making can be extremely fascinating. Granted that you are not an artist, and have little intention of trying to become one in this field, you will be surprised at the amount of real skill and artistry that will flow from your fingers as you continue to make dolls. There are so many reasons for making dolls, other than that of supplying your own or your relatives' children with engaging playthings. They can be mementoes of important occasions, a happy relief from constant mending and darning, and a pleasure "because you love fine sewing." Once you start, you'll find your own reasons for making more than the number the little girl of the family really needs.

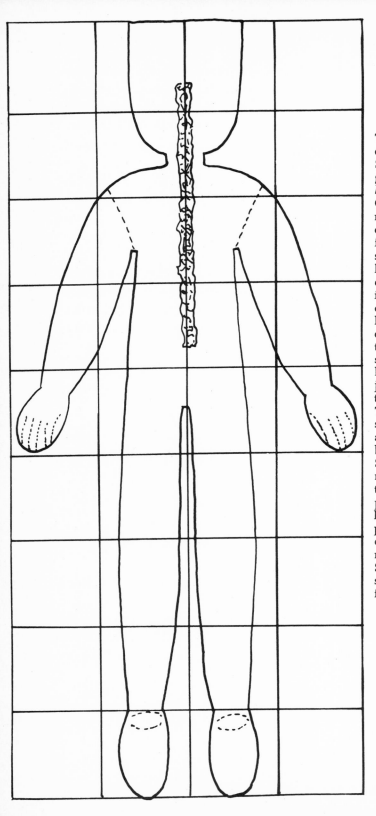

BASIC RAG DOLL PATTERN

The outline of the doll indicates the stitching line. Sew doubled fabric together along this line *before* cutting out doll. Overcasting seams at neck, underarms and crotch helps eliminate fraying when turned inside out. Leave top of head open, and opening on left side of about 2 inches a little below underarm, for stuffing. Stuff legs first, then arms to dotted lines. Stitch along these lines. You may also stitch across knees or hip line if you want more joints in doll. Stuff body to shoulders. Sew up side. Through top of head insert a pipe stem cleaner as shown, centering it in body as much as possible. Stuff all around it and almost to top of head. Close top by folding and lapping material to round off head. Features may be painted or embroidered on. Simulate fingers by means of small stitches. Sew curved lines of instep together to draw up feet into more natural position.

On the following pages are basic patterns for rag-doll bodies and limbs. They are of the utmost simplicity, but you may make them as elaborate and realistic as you choose. Indeed, simplicity is the first secret of good doll making, as it is in most other handicrafts.

Do not think that the smallest size doll is necessarily the easiest to make. On the contrary, it is usually the most difficult. The eight- or twelve-inch size is the best to start with. After successfully making one or more of these, the smaller sizes may be tried. These "tinies" should be entirely sewed by hand in order to follow accurately the much smaller curves. Machine sewing may be used for the larger dolls.

The doll patterns are given on "squared-off" pages so that you may enlarge or diminish them for your own requirements. It is very easy to scale these patterns to the size you want. Notice that each square is a perfect one. If you maintain the same accuracy, you will have no difficulty in changing the size of the pattern.

HOW TO SCALE A PATTERN TO SPECIFIC SIZES

To make the doll pattern larger, trace the pattern you wish to enlarge, including the squared-off lines, on a large sheet of paper, making the tracing in the lower left-hand corner. Starting at the lower left-hand corner of the tracing, place a ruler diagonally across the tracing so that the ruler's edge touches both the lower left-hand corner and the upper right-hand corner. Draw a line along the ruler carrying it out much further than the tracing. Now, extend the bottom line of the tracing across to the right for some distance.

If you wish to make the pattern 12 inches high, place the ruler in a vertical position on the bottom line and run it along until the distance between the bottom and the diagonal line is exactly 12 inches. Draw a line between these two points. Draw in the top line. Be sure that these boundary lines all join each other at perfect right angles.

Count the number of squares on the tracing, both horizontally and vertically. Measure off the same number of divisions on the enlarged rectangle, but make them larger in the proportion that the original tracing bears to the desired size. Draw in the lines. With this enlarged squared-off background, it is easy to draw in the outlines of the pattern, using the individual squares to show just exactly where individual curves and parts should fall.

To make the pattern smaller than shown in the sketch, you simply reverse the procedure. It is doubtful, however, that you will want to make this type of doll body any smaller than shown.

USING THE PATTERN

Once you have drafted a pattern of the desired size, either by enlarging or tracing the actual size shown in the sketches, it is a good idea to transfer the pattern to a piece of light-weight cardboard or construction paper. This makes a more permanent pattern, which may be used many, many times. It is also easier to use than a flimsy paper one. Cut the master pattern from the construction paper or cardboard, taking care to cut along the drawn line. Now place the cut out pattern on doubled fabric, which has been pinned or basted together to prevent slipping. With a soft pencil, trace around the paper pattern, making sure that the pencil point never swings away from the edge of the pattern.

Do not bear down on the pencil too heavily, for that will drag and wrinkle the fabric. If the material seems difficult to get a drawn line on, stroke the pencil rather than try to make a continuous line. When you have marked the entire outline of the pattern on the fabric, lift off the pattern. Keep the doubled pieces pinned or basted together while you do the sewing.

SEWING THE PIECES TOGETHER

Do not cut out the shapes drawn from the pattern!

Stitch first, either by hand or by machine, along the outside drawn lines. An opening of 2 inches or less is left on the left side seam to be used to stuff the parts. The top of the head is also left open. The stitches should be firm and close together. Use back stitch for the hand-sewn body; but do not pull the thread too tight.

SUSIE AND ISHKABIBBLE

Here is an engaging pair of rag dolls in the doll-house doll size. Susie is 6 inches tall, her brother only 4 inches high. They are made from the basic doll pattern. The boy's pajamas are pink and white check. Susie's dress, dark blue plaid.

After the necessary stitching has been completed, cut out the shapes with very sharp scissors. The line of cutting should be, for dolls up to 12 inches in height, not more than an eighth of an inch outside the stitching. On very small dolls, a sixteenth of an inch is better. Turn the parts inside out.

STUFFING THE DOLL

The doll stuffed carefully and well will look better and last longer than one done carelessly. The material used for stuffing is dependent somewhat upon the ultimate purpose of the doll. Light-weight material is always desirable, especially for use by young children. Cotton batting, kapok or cotton flock are all good. On the other hand, if the body material is very firm and closely woven, and the doll is intended for an older child, ordinary sawdust, obtained from a local sawmill, serves very well. The sawdust is free and, if you tell the miller what you want it for, he will save clean sawdust for you.

Use small quantities of stuffing at a time. Avoid a lumpy look by smoothing and fitting the pieces carefully as they are pushed into place. A thin wooden dowel, a wood lollypop stick, or a wood meat skewer, all may be used to push down and adjust the stuffing. Work the stuffing into the curves and corners so that they are plump and evenly filled out. The finished work should be quite firm without distorting the outlines or stretching the fabric.

If you want a semblance of a jointed appearance for the rag doll, stitch it at the right places—at the knees, the hips and the shoulders. Stitching should be done before stuffing is completed. When you have stuffed leg up to knee, stop to stitch across knee joint. Same goes for hips and shoulders. The shoulder stitching should be a nearly vertical line, from top of shoulder to armpit. The knee and hip stitching is horizontal. All rag dolls require some form of stiffening in the neck to keep the head from flopping over. A short piece of thin wooden dowel does the trick nicely. This should be centered, with the stuffing worked around it. Place the dowel so that at least one-third of its length is up inside the doll's head.

FINISHING THE DOLL

The next step is to sew the openings together. You do this with close fine stitches. Turn one edge in and hem it to the other side. A curved line may be given the hands by stitching a small tuck on the inside of each wrist. The feet may be turned up to look more natural by taking a larger tuck across the top of the foot at about the point where a real ankle would be. While this may be done before stuffing, it is easier to do it afterwards. The effect of fingers may also be given by putting in tiny lines of stitching from the tip of the hand back a slight distance. This must be done on the right side after the stuffing has been completed.

FACE AND HAIR

Hair and features are the last finishing touches. It is better to put on the hair before doing anything about the eyes and mouth. Most people tend to put these features up too high on the face. You can avoid this error by putting them in on the face when the hair-do is completed, for the hair-line forces the eyes down to the proper points for placing the features.

Ways of making hair for rag dolls are given on pages 20-21. Features may be embroidered or painted on. When embroidering, lightly pencil guide lines for the needle to follow. Suggest rather than attempt a completely accurate and realistic representation of the eyes and mouth. Very attractive and often amusing results are obtained by appliquéd features. Designs for these are also given on page 26. Painting is most satisfactorily done with pigments designed especially for use on fabrics. Experiment with them on a piece of scrap material before actually beginning a doll face. Use a very fine pointed sable water-color brush for painting the features.

A MOLDED FACE FOR A RAG DOLL

Sooner or later the desire to make a doll face with three-dimensional or molded features will become stronger and stronger. It

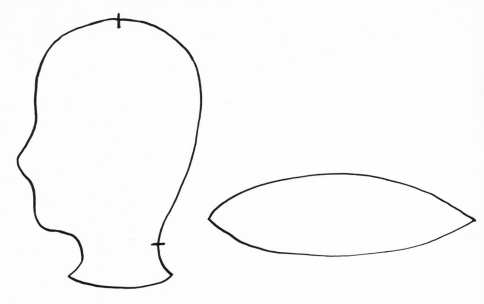

PROFILE FACE FOR A RAG DOLL

Two pieces of fabric are cut as shown. The size is dependent upon the size of the head. Trace or draw a similarly proportioned profile, and transfer it to a double piece of material. Stitch along the drawn profile *before cutting it out*. Leave back of head open. Cut out head about ⅛ inch from stitching along front. Allow ¼ inch for back seams. Sew pointed oval gusset in back from A to B. Sew back of neck together. Stuff head tightly.

YARN HAIR-DOS

Many variations may be worked with knitting yarn hair-dos. For upswept styles, sew the strands of wool along the natural hair line of the face. They must completely encircle the head. Work with long pieces that are bent in half. Sew bend to head, centering it over one end of preceding piece. The long strands may be drawn up and twisted into a bun, arranged in curls (made by wetting the yarn and wrapping it around a knitting needle; let dry) or formed into ringlets that are tacked down.

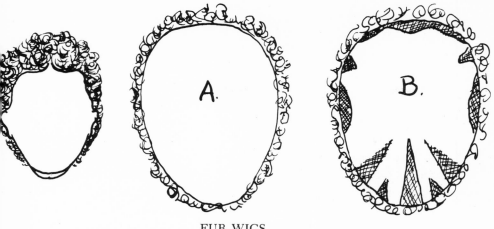

FUR WIGS

Cut an oval from fur that is as long as distance from forehead to nape of neck, and is as wide as from ear to ear around back of head. Use a razor blade to cut out shaded areas as indicated. Fit to doll's head so that sections meet each other. Make necessary adjustments. Coat skin side of fur with cement, fit on doll, hold down with kerchief to dry.

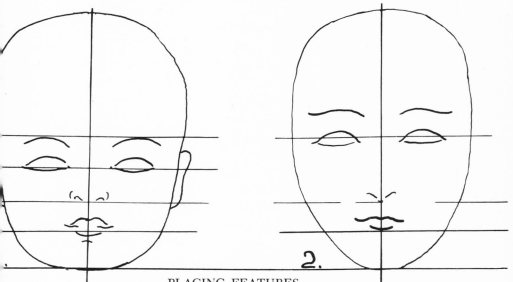

PLACING FEATURES

The correct placing of the features on a doll's head indicates the approximate age it is supposed to represent. The size of the head need not be changed. Picture at left shows how the head is divided to make an infant's or very young child's face. The oval is divided in half, the lower part of which is then divided into four equal parts. Notice how the top of the eyebrows just touches the half-way line and how the rest of the features fall at the other sub-division lines. Picture at right shows an adult face in which the half-way line goes through the center of the eyes. The lower half of the face is again divided and this line indicates the position of the bottom of the nose. The effect of adultness may be increased by making the head more slender through the forehead than is characteristic of the child.

is not difficult to make and requires patience rather than artistic skill. You need few and simple materials.

Wigless Bisque Doll's Head Makes a Fine Model. While any type of doll's head may be used as a model for making a doll's face, a bisque one is preferable because it has such well-defined features. This is important because the process of making a molded face, actually a mask, tends to blur and smooth out small characteristic details. Also important is the fact that the bisque head is quite unharmed by the process while other doll head materials may have their surfaces marred when the mask is removed.

The materials required for the initial mask are thin cotton jersey (a man's T-shirt works well) and a liquid that will dry hard. Wallpaper paste or plaster of Paris, each mixed with water to the consistency of thin cream, may be used. Either is a matter of choice. However, if plaster of Paris is used it will be necessary to work rather quickly as it starts hardening quite rapidly.

For a bisque head measuring about 5 inches from chin to hairline, cut a square of the jersey about 12 inches each way. Dip the jersey into the liquid, then hold it up to allow excess to run off. Place the saturated fabric on the doll's face and, starting at the bridge of the nose, smooth it into all crevices and indentations, stretching it where necessary to eliminate wrinkles. The grain of the fabric should run up and down. Work quickly and rub the fabric down firmly and smoothly so that every bit of it adheres to the bisque. Use the fingernails to sharpen indentations around the eye sockets and nostrils. If the bisque lips are slightly open make a short horizontal slit in the fabric to facilitate shaping the lips.

The under-chin and neck section requires gentle coaxing and stretching to get a wrinkle-free fit. If absolutely necessary, the fabric may be slit vertically and narrow darts cut out to achieve a smooth fit. The cut edges must be worked together, not overlapped. Only the front half of the bisque model is masked. See photograph on page 23. Cut excess fabric away. Let the mask dry for at least 24 hours, longer in damp weather. When quite

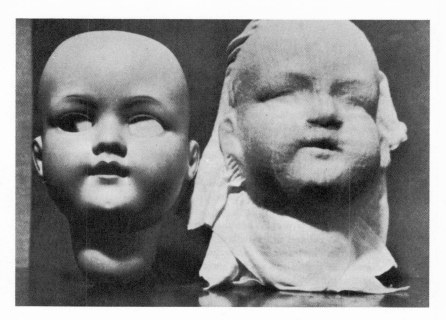

MAKING A MOLDED FACE

Bisque head and the first step in making a molded face from it. The author used loosely woven muslin and wallpaper paste solution.

dry the mask is ready to be brought to life by having its skin put on. This is both an exciting and a challenging operation.

Putting on the Skin. A variety of materials may be chosen to make the skin for the doll's face; the same thin cotton jersey, silk crepe, chiffon, thin dress muslin or an old, man's size linen handkerchief are all quite workable. Nylon hose may also serve providing it is the proper color. Do not expect to find a dress fabric in the right shade. Experiment with dyes, choosing a pale beige to start with, or dip the material in a medium strong brewing of tea. Remember that the color will dry lighter than it looks while wet and the desired tone is a honey beige with the faintest possible flush of pink enlivening it. Iron the fabric carefully when it is dry.

In the case of woven fabrics a desirable amount of stretch is possible by using it on the bias. The grain of knitted fabrics must run up and down and when used for skin should have the wrong side out. Of course the ultimate character of the doll plays a large part in the color of its complexion. Bisque heads are always quite pretty and childish; however, various racial strains can be suggested by complexion color (and hair). Decide before applying the skin.

While the mask is still on the head, brush a thin even coat of diluted (half and half) Elmer's or Sobo's glue over every bit of it. Apply the skin in the same manner as before, starting at the bridge of the nose. Work quickly and smoothly. Dip your fingertips in water to facilitate smoothing. If the complexion fabric is very thin some of the glue will seep through to the surface. Rub it away with wet fingers. It will be invisible when dry.

When the second cover or skin is perfectly dry the features may be painted on using either artist's oils or textile paints. Begin with the eyes and paint the eye sockets white. The irises should be larger than life and directed slightly to one side. It is almost impossible for an amateur to paint eyes looking directly ahead and have them turn out the same size. Use a light rose color for the lips and a lighter tone of it for the cheeks. However, do not paint the cheeks with a brush. Use your fingertips and lightly rub it on, shading it out towards the ears. Delicately feather on the doll's brows using a light brown color. A most delicate line of the same brown may be drawn along the edge of the upper eyelid. A minute triangle of white may be put on each iris starting from the center to outside. Be sure they match in size and position.

When the painted features have dried loosen the edge of the mask with a silver table knife. Work gently and coax rather than pry it off. If desired, two or three coats of shellac may be brushed on the inside of the mask to strengthen it.

The body pattern (including the head) on page 29, enlarged to measure 16 inches from crotch to top of shoulder, would be good for a molded doll face such as you've just made. When stuffing body and head be sure to put in a wooden dowel extending from the top seam down through the neck and well into the chest. The mask is attached to the stuffed head.

Before putting on the mask stuff the inside of its cheeks, nose, forehead and chin so that a smooth concave inner surface is obtained. Try the mask on the head to see how long or short to set its neck. Very young children have quite short necks. When satisfied take off the mask and brush a generous coat of slightly diluted Elmer's on the front part of the stuffed head. Replace the mask and force the head from the back into the mask to assure complete contact with it. Bind it in place with bandaging or ribbon and allow it to dry. When dry, catstitch down the edge of the mask to the stuffed head.

Wigging and dressing the molded face doll is a special joy. Take your time and plan carefully. It might turn into a charming duplicate of your own child at three or four years of age or it might . . . but that's the great satisfaction in doll making.

SIMPLE SIMON RAG DOLL

A Simple Simon rag doll is an excellent project for a beginner, and always fun for the experienced maker of dolls. The pattern shown may be traced off and transferred to fabric, or enlarged. Cut body, arms and neck from doubled material, and stitch along the drawn line. Leave necessary seam allowance when cutting. The head requires two pieces. To increase the roundness, a narrow strip of the material cut on the bias may be sewed between back and front of head. Leave an open space at top for stuffing.

The features, put on before stuffing, are appliquéd on. A half-circle of white is first appliquéd in place. A smaller circle of either blue or brown is then appliquéd to make the iris. A tiny pin circle makes the nose and a crescent of deep pink makes the mouth.

Make the sole and top of shoe of dark felt to get a striking shoe effect. Sew top to sole, stitch up back, slip-stitch to bottom of leg. (In this stitch the edges meet flat together, without any turning inside out, as in regular seams.) Now the stuffing begins. With kapok or flock or cotton batting, firmly stuff first one leg, then the other. Proceed with body up to armpits. Now stuff the arms but only to line from armpits to shoulder. Seam across this line on each arm. After both arms are done, fill rest of body to shoulders. Sew up shoulders.

Force a wooden skewer down through neck well into body stuffing. This will keep neck rigid, head from falling forward. Stuff neck only half way up, making sure to surround top part

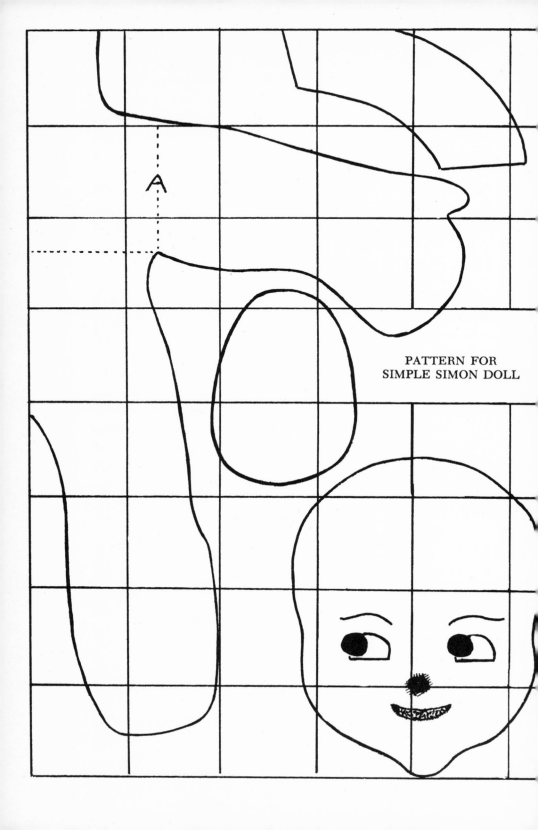

A

PATTERN FOR
SIMPLE SIMON DOLL

of skewer with cotton. Rest of neck is sewn flat to back of head, which is placed rather far down on neck. If there is any tendency to wobbliness of head, further reinforce it by means of a pipestem cleaner slipped down middle of neck flap and then slip-stitched up back of head to top.

Make hair of rug yarn, knitting wool, fur or sheepskin, as described on pages 20-21.

BONNIE, THE DOLL WITH MOLDED FACE

Shown in the photograph on page 28, Bonnie is almost as large as a three-year-old child. She takes no longer to make than a smaller doll does. Her molded face (instructions on page 19) is of light peach felt painted with textile paints. Arms and hands are of matching felt. Body and legs are of matching cotton flannel. She is stuffed with cotton flock, which is much less expensive to use for a doll this size than other types of stuffing.

The pattern for Bonnie's body, as shown, calls for a head cut in one piece with the body. The molded face is fitted to the front of this head. A thick padding of flock is inserted between inner side of face and front of head before the sewing-on of the molded face is completed. The outline of the body, arms and legs is the sewing line. Make seam allowance when cutting.

Body A. Fold two pieces of material lengthwise and cut as shown. (When unfolded, they make front and back.) Cut a bias strip 1½ inches wide and long enough to go up both sides and over top of head. Sew this bias strip between front and back, but not along bottom. This strip gives roundness to doll body. Shaded area: dart and seamed up for nipping in waistline.

B. Oval piece for bottom of body. Fold material in half, first horizontally, then again vertically. Cut one oval.

Arm C. Cut 4 pieces from felt and overcast together on right side.

Leg D. Cut 4 pieces. Seam together leaving top, bottom open.

E. Cut 2 pieces. They make soles of feet.

27

BONNIE
Her molded face started with base mask shown on page 23. She is 28 inches tall.

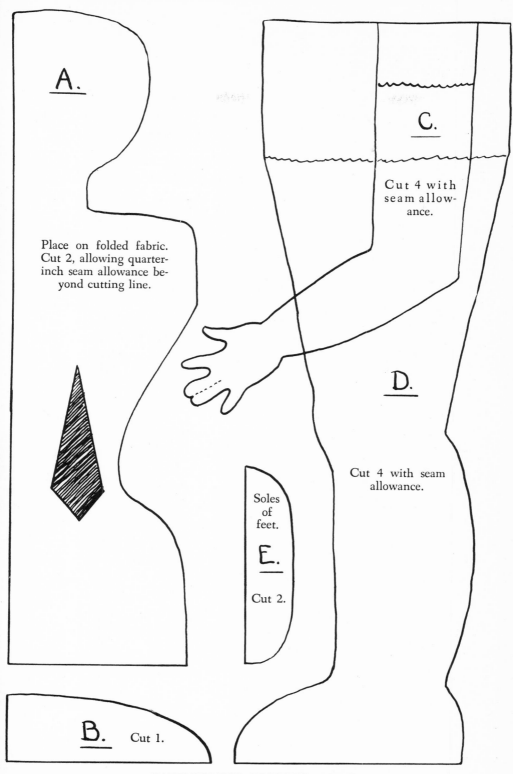

A.

Place on folded fabric. Cut 2, allowing quarter-inch seam allowance beyond cutting line.

C.

Cut 4 with seam allowance.

D.

Cut 4 with seam allowance.

Soles of feet.

E.

Cut 2.

B. Cut 1.

PATTERN FOR BONNIE'S BODY

Stuffing. Cotton flock or kapok. Stuff body through bottom; insert a wooden dowel in middle of neck and stuff around it firmly. Stuff legs from top, stopping at wavy line on pattern—excess material above is for sewing leg to body. Stuff arm from top, using but little in the hand, then quite firmly from above wrist to wavy line at top. Use tiny stitches to indicate closed fingers.

HOW TO MAKE A LENCI-TYPE DOLL

In the 1920's, a series of dolls was brought to this country from Italy. Made of felt and having exquisite clothes, their faces had an endearing charm and appeal. Wide-eyed and wistful, with tiny rosebud mouths, the Lenci doll face was immediately recognized as the work of an artist of taste and imagination. The Lenci dolls became quite popular, considering the comparatively high price charged for them.

To bring the Lenci dolls within the reach of a wider public, they were later made with cloth bodies and less elaborate costumes. Attractive as these cheaper dolls were, they did not equal the previous group. The originals had been designed and made by Madame Lenci (Di E. Scavini) of Turin, Italy. The first patent was taken out in September, 1921. They were manufactured until the mid-30's.

Inspired by the childish contours of the Lenci doll legs and arms, the accompanying pattern gives a similar effect of round youthfulness. Use pale beige or light peach all-wool felt for the legs and arms, and matching muslin for the body. All sewing is done along the drawn lines. The felt is slip-stitched together (the edges meeting flat) instead of regular seaming which requires turning inside out. The hands and fingers *must* be sewn this way.

Stuff very firmly. Allowance is made for a tab by which the arm is sewed to the shoulder. The legs may be done the same way; however, they become movable if attached by means of a button at each side. Use a very long darning needle and push it straight through body from side to side. Strong carpet thread should be used.

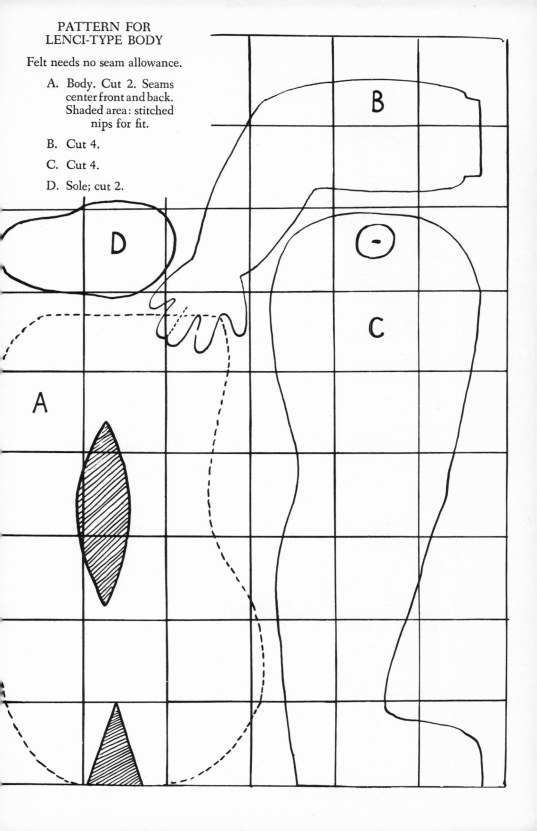

PATTERN FOR
LENCI-TYPE BODY

Felt needs no seam allowance.

A. Body. Cut 2. Seams
center front and back.
Shaded area: stitched
nips for fit.

B. Cut 4.

C. Cut 4.

D. Sole; cut 2.

B

D

C

A

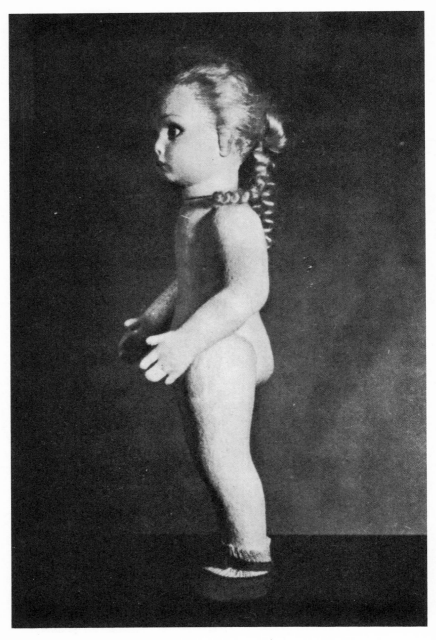

AN ORIGINAL LENCI DOLL, c. 1928, MADE ENTIRELY OF FELT
Body pattern on page 31 closely approximates her shape and proportions.

The head which you use for this body is a matter of choice. In size it should be no longer than 2½ inches from top of head to chin. Make it of composition, papier-mâché, fired ceramic clay or just a rag-doll head. Chapter 6 tells you how to make these composition heads.

Lenci dolls were not only made of felt, but the main parts of their costumes were felt. If you turn to Chapter 12, you will find a picture of a dressed Lenci doll, with some inspiring ideas for designing and trimming costumes.

HOW TO MAKE AND DRESS MARY LOU

Mary Lou, whose picture is on the frontispiece, is 10 inches high and is made from the basic rag-doll pattern on page 14. She has a sprinkling of tiny freckles (minute stitches made with fine brown thread) across her face. That is always an effective device to give expression and appeal to a flat-face rag doll. Her hair is made of pale yellow zephyr yarn, put on as shown on page 20. The ends are curled up by wetting them and rolling them up on a knitting needle. Slip out needle and hold the loops by means of a bobby pin slipped through them. The patterns shown are of dress details, in actual size. No seam allowance shown.

Underwear. Tiny panties are cut as shown in the diagram. Material is cut double, having the fold at the bottom. Top is shirred into a straight band that fits the waist. The petticoat, fitted to a narrow waist band, is 12 inches wide and 6 inches deep, hemmed and tucked to desired length. Both panties and petticoat are trimmed with very narrow lace.

Dress. Bodice of dress is cut as shown at A. Fold of material is at top to form shoulders. Smallest size ric-rac is used for trim. The skirt, measuring 14 inches around the hem, is cut to desired length and shirred onto bottom of bodice.

Slippers. Cut from moss green felt, the tops of the slippers C are sewn to soles D, then sewn up the back. A narrow strip, long

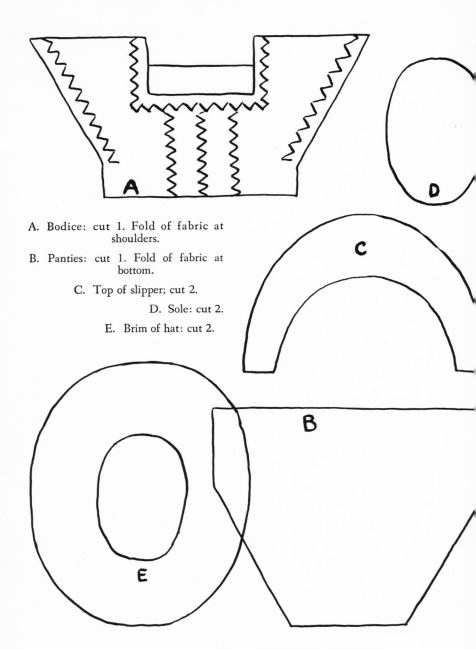

A. Bodice: cut 1. Fold of fabric at shoulders.

B. Panties: cut 1. Fold of fabric at bottom.

C. Top of slipper; cut 2.

D. Sole: cut 2.

E. Brim of hat: cut 2.

PATTERN FOR MARY LOU'S COSTUME

Boy doll from Mary Lou pattern. Changes
in hair-do and features emphasize character.
Shirt: fold line of fabric across shoulders.
Pants: fold line of fabric along straight
vertical edge of pattern. Cut 2. Seam long
diagonal of each piece together (legs). Seam
short diagonal of one leg to matching diagonal of other leg, front and back.

SUSPENDERS
AND BIB

BOY DOLL

BOY'S SHIRT OR JACKET

LONG PANTS

enough to go around the ankles, and lap over a little, is sewn to center back of each slipper.

Hat. Two pieces of material are cut as shown at E, cutting out the shaded area. The pieces are sewn together around the outer edge, turned inside out, pressed and then basted together around inside edge. A narrow bias strip is sewed around inside edge to finish it. This strip will stand up when a piece of narrow ric-rac is slip-stitched to it. Put on head and pin with pearl-headed pins.

MARY LOU BECOMES A CHARMING MOTHER

A small bead between stuffing and face covering makes a tiny nose. Child is a roll of cotton tied at neckline for head. Yellow silk French knots make hair. Author made Virgin and Child for a Christmas Crèche which included Joseph (same pattern) and a small shepherd (reduced pattern).

2.

How to Make More
Advanced Dolls

*T*HIS TYPE OF DOLL CLOSELY APPROXIMATES THE ROUNDED human figure. It is built up on a wire frame or skeleton which is wrapped to "flesh" it. The outer covering or "skin" may be made by wrapping with narrow strips of soft material, wrapping with 4-ply knitting wool, or inserting the body into a casing that has been cut and sewed to size and shape. Since this type of doll will be more elaborately dressed than is the child-doll, keep the waist-line on the tiny side. An exaggeratedly small waist means that the costumes will look better and smarter, since the fullness of the skirts will set more successfully. A thick body-line produces a thick, chunky and ungraceful costume.

A WIRE FRAME FOR THE DOLL

The doll's skeleton, as shown on page 38, may be made of pipe stem cleaners, or copper wire as shown, of no. 18 or no. 20 gauge. The doll stands beside a "lay figure," or artists' model in human proportions, for comparison. Notice that the wire loop which in-

37

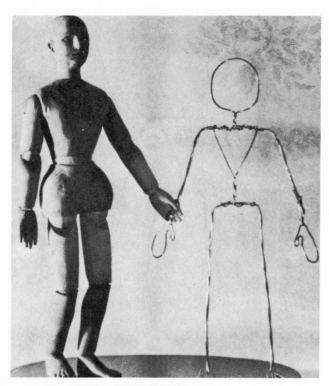

WIRE FRAME
FOR THE DOLL

Showing compari-
son of proportions
with the normal
figure.

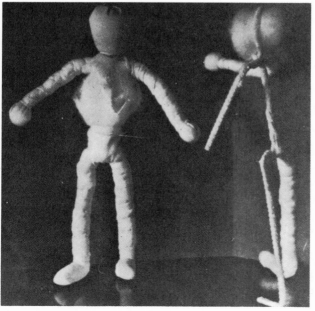

PIPE STEM
CLEANER
FRAMES

Two stages of pad-
ding the frames
with cotton, and
wrapping evenly
over padding. Ny-
lon hose, cut to fit
arms and legs, is
fitted smoothly and
slip-stitched up
back of each leg.

dicates the head is larger than that of the lay figure; the arms are somewhat longer and the wire pelvis higher in proportion. These exaggerations are desirable in doll making, although care should be taken not to carry the exaggeration too far. Keep in mind the fact that the lay figure approximates the human *adult* figure, wherein the head is smaller in proportion to the rest of the body than is true of children.

Avoid using too stiff a wire, since that adds unnecessary difficulties in shaping, without benefiting the finished doll. Too soft a wire is equally undesirable, since the purpose of the skeleton is to maintain rigidity, support the doll on its feet and yet be pliable enough to permit the body and limbs to be bent into various poses.

Using a Pipe-Cleaner Frame. The photograph on page 38 illustrates two steps in the making of a doll on a pipe-cleaner frame. The right-hand figure shows the skeleton with cotton wound around one arm and leg, and a ball of cotton held by the wire loop head. The left-hand figure shows the legs and arms covered with narrow strip wrappings, the head covered with a piece of material that has been drawn in at the neck and top of head to give a smooth and rounded face. The fitting of this piece of material at the back of the head is later covered by the hair.

Details that Add Charm to the Doll. By adding a few extra details to the doll, you can make it gain a good deal in character and effectiveness. It is quite easy to model various style shoes on the feet of this type of doll. With a little practice, credible-looking hands may also be modeled. When this sort of detail is planned for, do not put flesh and skin on the feet or hands. Allow enough wire at ends of legs and arms to bend into loops. The modeling medium (self-hardening clay, salt-cornstarch composition, or crack filler, etc.) is worked on the wire loops. Self-hardening clay is on sale at many stores. The salt-cornstarch solution is mixed (one part salt, two parts cornstarch) with one part boiling water. It is mixed, kneaded and pressed into shape desired. Crack filler is putty mixed with cold water to soften it like dough.

Begin with Simple Forms. Your first attempts should be simple forms merely suggesting the desired shapes. Later, as your hands become more adept in handling the clay, you may model actual shoes of various styles and hands with fingers. The self-hardening clay needs no moistening agent. Other types of modeling media, when home mixed, should be pliable but not sloppy. Be sure the feet have been pressed down firmly on a flat surface to make their soles even, so that, when dry, the doll will stand up. Still later, the entire leg to just below the knee, the arm to the elbow, may be modeled and painted.

Two Ways to Form the Nose. The effect of a nose may be added in two ways. Instead of using a flat piece of material and molding it around the head, cut a double piece of fabric according to the pattern on page 20. As you can see, the effect of a profile is achieved. This, of course, means that the face will have a center seam. When stuffing has been firmly placed within the head, the center seam gives a decided nose to the rag-doll face. The sewing of the seam must be quite strong, with the stitches very closely set.

The other method of endowing the face with a nose is to roll a bit of clay or plastic wood into the shape and size of the desired nose. Let it dry. Attach it to the front of the doll's head with a drop of cement. Naturally, you should do this before the face covering is put on. When cement is dry, cover the face as usual. A few tiny stitches at bridge and nostrils will mold the material down, thus accenting the nose.

Needle Modeling the Face. A good deal of expression may be given the usual flat-faced rag doll by means of needle modeling. This consists of nothing more difficult than setting a few tiny stitches at strategic points. The needle is pushed through from the back of the head to come out at the front at the desired point. The needle tip is reinserted directly beside the place it emerged from, is pushed through to back of the head and drawn out. By tightening the thread, the indentation on the face may be adjusted to the desired depth.

HELMI, A GAY OLD COUNTRY WOMAN, PROJECTS REAL CHARM

Needle modeling and a sense of humor endow this rugged old country woman made in 1960 with considerable charm and personality. The front half of the head was partially stuffed, then small pieces of cotton were placed on outside at strategic points and tacked in place to get desired form and plumpness. In each instance the forms were exaggerated to allow for compression by the nylon hose skin. It too was tacked down. Eyes were emphasized by back-stitching to create lids. Sockets were painted black and shiny black beads forced in and glued. After lips were painted a thin strip of white wool was forced between them to simulate teeth. Cheeks, nose and chin had deep rose paint rubbed on. White lamb's wool hair, glued on, and white bead earrings accentuate her tanned complexion. Body is muslin stuffed with cotton with wire inserts in arms and legs. Hands, formed with wire, are mitt-shaped.

COMPLEXIONS

Since this more elaborate type of rag doll is designed for costume or collector's pieces, it may have an especially fine complexion if desired. After needle modeling or nosing, or both, the face may be covered with chiffon (this stretches nicely), sheer nylon or silk hose, even very thin beige or white leather (taken from old kid or suede evening gloves). When planning this sort of face, draw the features on the original face (thin covering over the stuffing) with pencil. Needle model at desired points, then stretch on the new complexion. This, too, with the exception of thin leathers, must have a few extremely tiny stitches, taken at the modeled points, to anchor the new complexion to the face. The features are then painted on.

Glue and Orange Stick. Leather complexions may be pasted on with vegetable glue. This is rubbed all over the back or wrong side of the leather, which is then placed on the face and gently rubbed down. Using the blunt end of an orange stick, rub it delicately into the indentations formed by the needle modeling. You have to do this to form a contact between the kid and the underface. Naturally, the thinner the leather, the more easily it may be worked. If the kidskin seems too heavy, try scraping it with a very sharp penknife or any knife having a rounded blade. The scraping is done on the wrong side, working only a small area at a time.

FORMING THE EYES, NOSE AND MOUTH

The proper placing of these important features requires a good deal of care. The inexperienced doll maker, as we have noted, always tends to place the features too high up on the face, giving it an old, pinched and wizened look. On page 21 you will find a pair of ovals representing faces. The horizontal lines crossing these ovals indicate the points where the eyebrows, eyes, bottom of nose and center line of mouth should be located. The center vertical line indicates the middle point of the face. Study them. Make a few rough sketches of your own. Learn to control the impulse to work high on the face rather than low.

The Eyes are Important. It is always better to make the eyes too large. Small eyes give a mean, suspicious look to the face. Set them evenly on either side of the vertical line, allowing a space

HELMI'S TRAVELLING SUIT FITS HER PERSONALITY

No fashion queen, Helmi wears a rough tweed skirt, cotton blouse and scarf and felt jacket, which look just right on this jolly country woman. Her only concession to style is the felt hat and matching bag.

equal to the width of one eye to separate them. Noses, on the perfectly flat face, need not be indicated at all. A fine sprinkling of freckles—minute scattered stitches made with dark brown thread—add piquancy and youth to a doll's face. Keep them high up, starting at about where the bridge of the nose would be if the doll really had a nose.

Not too Heavy Eyelashes. Eyelashes are usually effective if they are delicately made. They are needed only on the upper lid. Use tiny lines to indicate them and space them quite definitely. When too thickly used, they become a dark, heavy, unattractive smudge above the eyes.

The Lips Can Be Expressive. The mouth is a controversial feature. Some like it large. Some like it small. A full lower lip or the merest suggestion of one is a matter of personal taste. Full and rather pouting lips are indicative of very young children. The width of the mouth, for a young child's face, should be no wider than the flare of the nostrils. Since dolls of this type do not have obvious or discernible nostrils, it is a good idea to make the mouth only as wide as an eye.

It is really a mistake to try to make any feature too realistic or accurate. If they are properly placed on the face and in proportion to it, the merest suggestion of the feature is enough. Skill in depicting them comes with practice. As you experiment you will find that the fewer lines used and the faster they are executed, the better the final result.

PERRAULT DOLLS *(opposite page)*

This Cinderella group of fabric dolls, made by Marie Perrault of Detroit during the 1920's, is the epitome of design and execution of the rag doll. Varying in height from 9 to 16½ inches, they are entirely made of cloth with silk satin faces and embroidered features. Their clothes are extraordinarily rich and embellished with the finest needlework. Hair is made of silk floss. Some of them, depending upon the effect the artist wished to achieve, have two-piece faces, i.e., a center seam which endows the head with a definite profile. What contributes so largely to their beauty is the perfect scaling and detailing of the costumes and their trimmings.

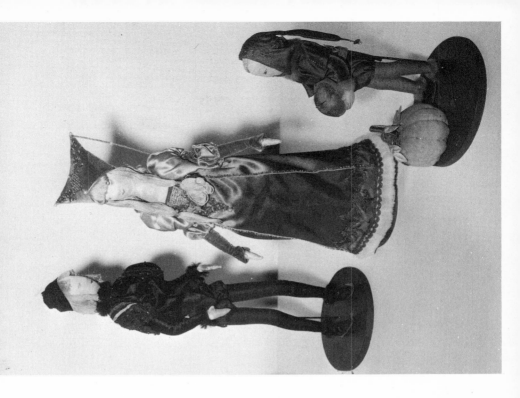

HAIR, WIGS, HEAD COVERINGS

A variety of materials may be used with which to simulate hair on rag dolls. Knitting yarn, rug wool, real hair, ten-cent-store switches, real wigs from doll hospitals, bits of sheepskin or Persian lamb or monkey fur, are some of them. Various styles of hair-dos, worked out with knitting wool or rug yarn, are shown on page 20. They tell their own story.

To use fur scraps, first cut out an oval of fur equal to the dimensions of the head from forehead to nape of neck, and from ear to ear. All cutting is done on the skin side of the fur with a razor blade. The oval is then slashed, as shown on page 21. The tiny pie-wedges that are removed make it possible to fit the fur onto the head without bulges. The skin side of the fur is coated with cement. It is fitted in place on the head of the doll and tied down with a piece of cloth, kerchief fashion, to hold the fur in place until the cement dries.

THE LEWIS AND CLARK EXPEDITION CARVED IN WOOD
(opposite page)

Ranging in size from 7 to 10 inches in height, this historical group created by Frances Bringloe of Seattle is outstanding for its completely authentic costumes as well as for expert carving. Many sources were studied to authenticate costume styling and details, including the actual journals of the expedition as well as the U. S. Government *Handbook of American Indians*. The making of an Indian girl doll sparked the idea which resulted in this fine museum-quality educational group. Padded wire frames were used for the bodies. The angle at which the photograph was taken makes the dolls look more short-legged than they actually are.

The characters depicted are, from left to right: Captain William Clark; his servant, York; Captain Meriwether Lewis; the Creole boatman Cruzatte; Sergeant Patrick Gass; the Shoshone chief Cameahwait; and his sister who guided the expedition, Sacajawea, with her baby born en route. The group is owned by the Detroit Children's Museum, a part of the city's public school system, and is used to dramatize American history.

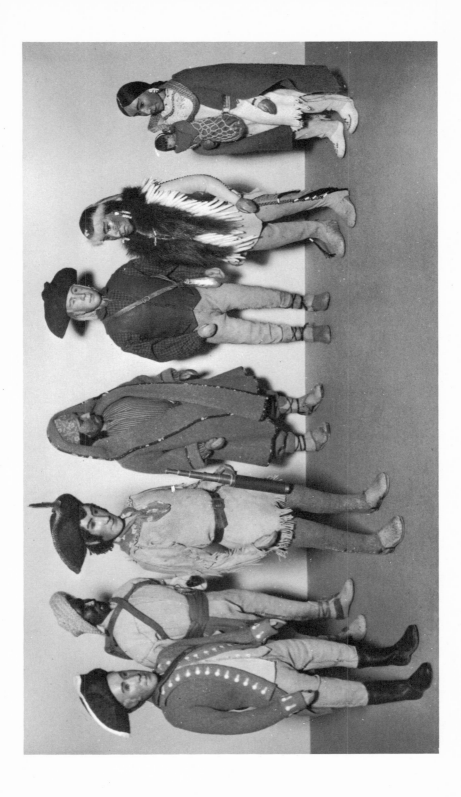

FINE PINK LUSTER DOLL

This doll is in perfect condition with original arms and legs and
white kid body. Found unclothed, she was dressed by the author in
white embroidered pique with tucked and embroidered underclothes
consisting of chemise, corset cover, drawers and three full petticoats. Costume was inspired by a daguerreotype of the period,
early 1860's.

3.

Dressmaking and Fancy Costume Designing for Dolls

$\mathcal{F}$ASCINATING AS IT IS TO CREATE AND MAKE A DOLL, IT IS even more fascinating to design clothes for it. The doll destined as a plaything for some little girl deserves just as much care and thought in dressing her as will be given to the more elaborate show or collector's doll. Naturally, the doll baby will be very simply dressed as compared with the gowns made for period and costume dolls. However, a basic rule applies to both types of dolls: everything must be kept in scale to the size of the doll! Attention to this important detail will produce dolls that are enchanting because of their perfection. Even very small children are aware of proportion and delicacy of workmanship although they cannot express themselves in those terms. You, yourself, will get much more enjoyment in making perfectly scaled doll clothes because you are meeting a challenge with the taste and skill of an artist.

The Different Doll Types. Doll dressmaking covers three types of dolls: the soft-bodied homemade rag doll, the hard-bodied commercial doll, and the antique doll whose body falls in hardness between the first two. There are as many different shapes in dolls' bodies as there are in people, and the sizes of dolls vary enormously. Consequently, it is quite impossible to give specific patterns for dresses and costumes that will cover all problems.

The patterns shown in the following pages are for specific dolls and may be used and adapted for dolls approximating the same measurements. The other illustrations shown are actually *shapes* to guide your own pattern cutting for individual problems.

THE SIZE OF THE DOLL DETERMINES THE CHOICE OF FABRIC AND TRIMMING

The most frequent source of doll's clothing—the rag-bag or piece box—too often fails to produce a patterned fabric of sufficiently *small design* to "look right" on the doll. The pattern or design of the material which was small on you frequently will look completely out of place on a small doll. When faced with this dilemma it is far better to choose a plain colored fabric, relying upon exquisite workmanship and simple trimming to give the dress distinction. Naturally, the same careful attention to the size of the trimming must be exerted or the dress will become coarse and commercial looking.

Choosing the Best Material. Cottons and silks that have been laundered will work up more easily, fall more gracefully on the doll. Heavy fabrics such as most woolens, velvets and velveteens should be confined to garments that do not require much fullness or draping as, in small garments, they are surprisingly unpliable. Wool jersey and wool crepe, however, are most satisfactory to work with. Old handkerchief linen is an ideal fabric for doll blouses and underwear. The majority of rayon fabrics are to be avoided because of their tendency to ravel easily.

Even with a wide range of colors to draw from it becomes tiresome to dress many dolls in plain-colored fabrics. If the search through remnant counters and other people's rag-bags is unproductive of exactly what you want to use, try transforming a plain fabric into a patterned one yourself.

NOTEWORTHY DETAILING OF COSTUMES

Thorough research and careful selection of fabrics make the costume of these historical dolls authentic. Robin Hood, made by Carolyn John, has carved wood head and hands and a soft wired body; he is 17 inches tall. General George Washington, by Bernard Ravca, also has a soft wired body. The hands and needle-sculptured face are of cloth with embroidered features.

How to Put Colored Designs on Plain Fabrics. There are two easy ways of endowing a plain fabric with colored designs. Simple enough to be in common use by grade school children, they offer little or no difficulty to the adult designer. The first and easiest method uses ordinary wax crayons. The second method employs paint which may be of three different types: special textile paints, artists' oil paints or ordinary poster or tempera paints. Your nine- or ten-year-old daughter can very probably tell you how *she* does it in school. Lacking a daughter to point out the techniques involved, just follow the simple directions below.

Steps in Color Designing. Any fabric to be decorated must first be ironed free of wrinkles. Spread it out flat on a drawing board or even a bread board using Scotch tape tabs to hold it in position. Suppose you want to make a series of colored stripes. With wax crayons and a ruler, draw the stripes on the fabric with a firm, even pressure. The width of the stripes may be controlled by the way the end of the crayon has been sharpened. A very fine point will give an equally fine line. To keep all the lines an even width, sharpen the crayon frequently. Wider stripe is made with a crayon that has been sharpened to a fairly thin but blunt end. The wider the end of the crayon, the wider will be the stripe. By combining thin and wide stripes alternately, or in definite groups, liveliness and character are added to the design.

There are many other ways of varying a striped design. Short blunt strokes radiating from either side of a thin line produce a stylized leaf pattern. Dots and small dashes placed diagonally between vertical stripes give still another pattern. Experiment, but always keep in mind the size of the doll for which the fabric is being prepared.

Use Care in Ironing. When the crayon design has been completed —and be sure to make enough of it so that there is plenty from which to cut the doll's gown—set the design by ironing it on the wrong side of the material with a fairly cool iron. Do not rub the iron back and forth. Set the iron down, press, then lift it to the next spot. Continue to do this until every bit of the crayoned

BOY OF 1850'S

HEIDI

53

KOREAN BOY

BALLET DANCERS

56

MEDIEVAL
PAGE BOY

design has been set. Surprisingly enough, materials so patterned can stand light laundering in cool water.

Painting Fabric Can Be Easy. The use of paint on fabric sounds as if it might be difficult. It really is not. Small-pointed sable brushes are used on a perfectly smooth fabric which is held down to a flat surface with Scotch tape. Full instructions for use are included with all textile paints. Artists' oil paints must be thinned a bit with turpentine. Poster or tempera paint is used just as it comes from the bottle but is definitely not recommended for use on a delicate fabric which will receive much handling. For display dolls, tempera paints will give a brilliant effect but will flake off if the material is subject to much movement. Textile and oil paints require at least twenty-four hours to dry before the material is handled. Poster paint dries much more quickly.

How to Experiment with Designs. If you do not trust your own artistic skill at first, make your initial experiments with voile, organdie, batiste or other semi-transparent fabrics. Lay the fabric over a design you have first drawn on paper, or over a small design taken from a book or magazine illustration or advertisement. It will show through the material and serve as a guide. A few experiments along these lines, with either crayons or paint, will give you sufficient confidence to branch out into free hand decoration. The trick to this type of fabric decoration is to keep the design small, simple and evenly spaced. Never let the motifs get too close together. Never try to make too *real* looking flowers or other objects. It is better to give a light suggestion of the design.

CUTTING OUT DOLL'S DRESSES AND COSTUMES

Dressmaking for dolls poses quite different problems than those met in making clothes for children or adults. The first and most obvious problem is that of size. In the following pages you will find the basic shapes of various parts of doll costumes. Their size and proportions must be adapted to fit the specific doll you are dressing. The easiest way of doing this is to cut the basic shape a bit larger than you think you will need, fit it to the doll and make the necessary adjustments.

How to Avoid Waste of Material. It is quite possible to waste material if this preliminary cutting and fitting is done directly in the fabric to be used. That can be avoided by cutting trial patterns out of cleansing tissue. It is soft, drapable and quite strong. It will hold pins or basting and will stand considerable handling. After the adjustments have been satisfactorily made, the tissue pattern may be smoothed out and used as a guide in cutting out the actual material.

Before You Cut. Think before you cut. Ask yourself the following questions before any cutting is done:

MIRANDA

A modern Penny Wooden dressed by the author. Blouse, pantalettes and petticoat are of sheer linen trimmed with bobbin lace. Pinafore is taffeta striped in gray, lavender and black. Batiste apron is hemstitched and finely embroidered.

How many seams can be eliminated in the making of the costume? The fewer seams there are, the less bulkiness there will be in the finished garment.

Are shoulder seams really necessary? Of course, folding the material along the shoulder answers the question, as is shown on page 63.

Do the sleeves have to be set in, or can they be cut in one with the blouse or bodice? Again, the one-piece method is shown as the easier way.

Does the skirt have to be in two or more pieces? Won't the same effect be gained by using one piece shirred to the necessary waistline and then placing the single joining seam either center front under an apron or at center back? The average doll wears the simple one-piece skirt gathered with more or less fullness to the waist. The exception is the gored or pleated model.

Will the doll be dressed and undressed—as it will if it is designed for a child's plaything—or will the clothes remain on the doll, once it has been completed? If it is a plaything, the doll's clothes must have openings and fastenings that are easily manipulated by the child. The best position for these openings is down the center back from the neckline to well below the waistline, thus giving plenty of room for taking off the dress without tearing it. Use the smallest-size snap fasteners to hold the frock together; sew them firmly, and show the child how easily they are opened by inserting the thumbnail between the top and bottom of the snap.

SEWING AND FINISHING THE DOLL'S DRESS

No matter how skillful one may be in working a sewing machine, the best doll's clothes and costumes are entirely handmade. While hand sewing may take more time, the final effect is so much prettier and in so much better scale that it is worth the extra effort involved. This is particularly true in finishing details of the garment such as tucks, hems for necklines and sleeves, etc. About the only place a line of machine sewing on a doll's dress is of advantage is when joining a full shirred skirt to a blouse or bodice.

MID-NINETEENTH CENTURY COMPOSITION HEAD DOLLS

Both dolls are about 30 inches tall with deep shoulder-heads of composition and exceptionally well-made cloth bodies. The right-hand doll wears original clothes, c. 1840. Her friend, c. 1855, wears a modern made dress created by her owner, Mrs. Ralph Sandt of Easton, Pa.

GODEY LADY DOLLS

Designed by Ruth Gibbs, Flemington, N. J., they were attractively dressed and packaged. Many thousands of them were sold in the 1940's.

Finishing Edges. With soft pliable fabrics make the tiniest of rolled hems to finish necklines and the bottoms of sleeves. Slightly heavier fabrics unsuited to rolling may be faced with silk tape which is sewn around the edge on the right side then turned in and pressed flat. Minute slip-stitches will hold the tape in position. Tiny ric-rac tape or braid used to trim the neckline will also keep the facing tape from slipping up into view.

Edges of Heavy Material. Velvet, velveteen and woolen fabrics always create a bulky and awkward line when they are hemmed back on themselves. Face skirt hems with matching silk. To finish the neckline and bottom of the sleeves of velvet or woolen frocks so that no lumpiness or bulging occurs is possible by means of tiny blanket stitching, or button-hole stitching, with matching thread. This is done on the wrong side of the material, spacing the stitches rather closely and making them quite short. When neatly done the blanket stitching is scarcely visible on the right side and it does what any hem is supposed to do—it prevents the fabric from raveling.

How to Press Tiny Seams. One of the big difficulties in getting a professional finish to a small doll's dress is that of ironing or pressing the work as it progresses. The average electric iron is much too large and a child's toy electric iron does not get hot enough to be effective on most fabrics. Some of this difficulty is sidestepped by making sure that every wrinkle has been ironed out before the actual sewing is begun. The wrinkles that occur during work and the necessity for pressing seams open can be taken care of by means of an electric curling iron! It can fit into the tiniest places and, with a rapid scissors motion, can be moved along fast enough to prevent it from pressing waves into the material. Since an electric curling iron does not have a heat control on it, test the degree of heat carefully before actually using. An off-on switch set a few inches below the handle of the iron is a simple job for your husband or son to do and having it will make the iron very much more convenient to use, if you turn your hobby into a vocation.

PATTERNS FOR BASIC BLOUSES

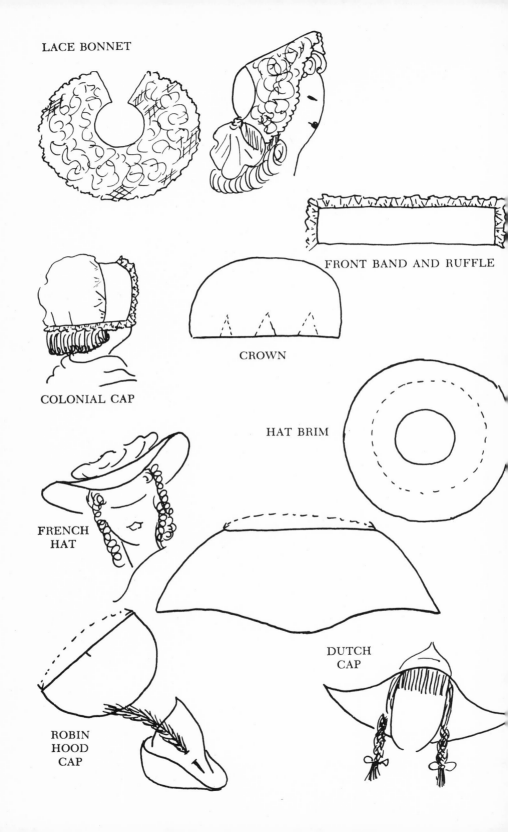

LACE BONNET

FRONT BAND AND RUFFLE

COLONIAL CAP

CROWN

HAT BRIM

FRENCH HAT

DUTCH CAP

ROBIN HOOD CAP

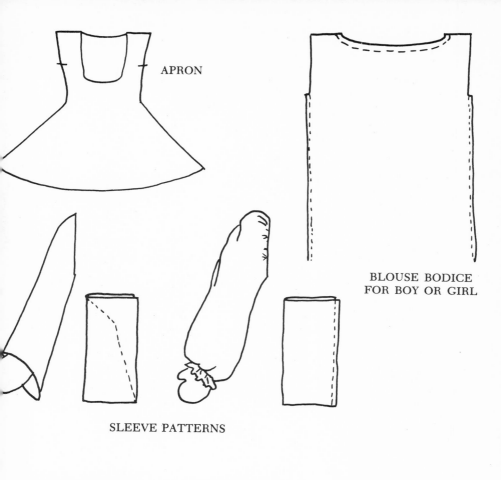

APRON

BLOUSE BODICE
FOR BOY OR GIRL

SLEEVE PATTERNS

SIC PATTERN FOR SHORT AND LONG TROUSERS

TYROLEAN BOY

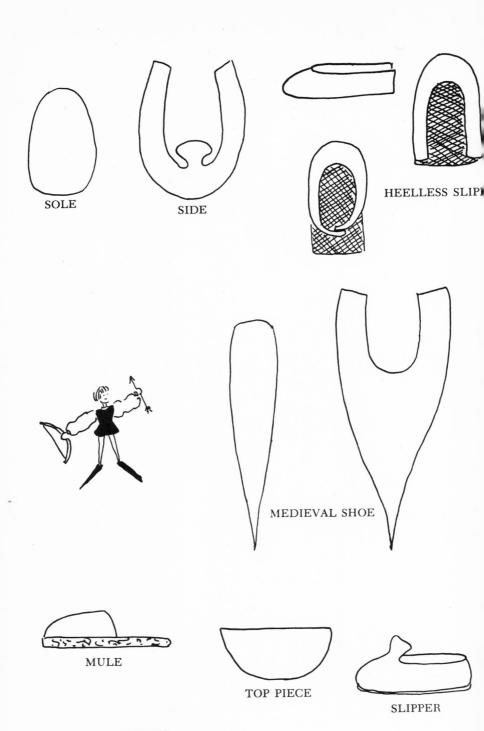

SOLE

SIDE

HEELLESS SLIPPER

MEDIEVAL SHOE

MULE

TOP PIECE

SLIPPER

SHOE PATTERNS

EFFECTIVE TRIMMING FOR DOLL'S CLOTHES

Once having started on the making of doll's clothes you will find yourself looking at practically everything in the departments of notions and dressmaking with an eye to its suitability for use on dolls. Don't, however, confine your attention to these two classifications. While you may find many interesting and perfectly scaled items, there are gratifying surprises in store for you when you venture into the radio, hardware, art supplies and toy departments!

The smallest ric-rac braid can be used to outline the neck or trim the bottom of the sleeves; it can be worked into decorative bands around the skirt, or used as belts and to accent pockets and trim hats. Very narrow soutache braid can be used in the same way. Frequently, however, it is difficult to find the right color soutache for a specific costume. Try making your own braid by tightly crocheting a chain of fine cord, thin wool, six-strand embroidery floss, cotton or silk. The chain is tacked on with matching thread and, because of its pliability, may be worked into most interesting patterns and designs.

Spaghetti tubing from the radio department may also be used to trim wool or velvet frocks. Since it is considerably stiffer than crocheted chain its use is confined to simple lines. It should be couched down with matching thread.

For Unusual Effects. The extremely fine copper and aluminum wire used for making coils for motors and radios becomes extremely effective when used as trimming on a doll's dress, particularly for peasant costumes and robes for kings and queens. It can actually be sewed through not too closely woven material. It can also be worked into spirals by winding it around a thin knitting needle. After the needle has been slipped out the spiral is flattened between the fingers and is then sewed to the costume. It can be used to simulate frogs and buttons. It can be used to thread tiny beads and will hold a string of them in desired shapes or swirls. Slightly heavier gauge copper and aluminum wire can be worked into jewelry with the aid of a needle-nose pliers.

DUTCH GIRL AND BOY

BLACK
FOREST
BRIDE

SWEDISH
GIRL

69

LAPLANDER

TYROLEAN GIRL

NORWEGIAN GIRL

70

The toy department will furnish all kinds and sizes of beads which may be put to effective use in trimming ornate costumes. Combined with wire, or used alone, beads add dramatic value to an otherwise simple costume.

Paint Your Trimming On. There is a special new plastic art paint that offers great possibilities for trimming and decorating doll costumes. The paint is forced out onto the fabric through a paper cone, similar to a pastry tube. With a little practice, really elaborate designs can be achieved with it. It comes in many colors as well as gold and silver, although I prefer to use gold and silver water-color paint for really delicate designs. It also has a colorless adhesive, used to hold down powdered metallic which comes in a variety of colors. For sparkle and glitter on crowns, circus and skating costumes, East Indian dancers, etc., this powdered metallic is most effective.

Wool Felt for Flowers and Trimmings. Colored wool felt, snipped into tiny motifs and designs which are sewed or pasted to the costume, is a trimming idea originated by Lenci (see photo on page 276) that has great charm and beauty. Tiny clusters of flowers may be made from felt and used for wreaths for the head or tucked into the belt or put into the hand of the doll. Such touches add interest and attractiveness to an otherwise static figure.

Old Stand-bys. Lace, of course, is a favored form of trimming. Narrow lace edgings may once again be obtained in five-and-dime stores. In selecting them choose both the simplest and the narrowest. These same stores also have very narrow velvet ribbon which may be used in a variety of ways to trim these miniature clothes.

Tiny buttons are usually hard to find although intensive search for them will prove rewarding. Wee pearl ones used on infants' old fashioned dresses are exactly right for a doll. Equally small buttons of a more decorative character are scarce and rather expensive. Extremely pretty buttons can be made from sealing wax! Tiny soft balls of the wax are molded between the fingers, flattened slightly to desired size and allowed to harden. They may be pasted on or,

RUSSIAN
PEASANT
DRESS

FIFTEENTH
CENTURY
LADY

73

what is more practical, sewed on. If the latter, holes must be pierced through the button, before it has hardened, with an oiled pin or needle. Very small highly colored beads may be pressed into the surface of the wax to give design interest.

Embroidery Is Lovely Trimming. Perhaps the most useful and gratifying form of trimming doll costumes is embroidery! No matter how ingenious and delightful a variety of applied trimmings may be, none of them can supplant and few of them can equal the delicacy and beauty of lovely embroidery. Since the garments are tiny ones, plans and designs for beautifying them with delicate stitchery may be much more elaborate than you'd care to go into for a full-size garment. A gown sprinkled with tiny embroidered floral sprays becomes enriched as it could in no other way.

A sheer cotton apron decorated with a band of colored embroidery like that worn by the doll on page 59 immediately becomes a collector's item. Incidentally, the apron, petticoat, pantalettes and blouse of this doll are of the sheerest linen, hemstitched (two threads drawn out) and pin tucked. One can afford both the time and effort for such exquisitely fine work because there is so little of it needed for a small wardrobe.

As one works with dolls it becomes more and more evident that here is a lifetime hobby of insistent interest and limitless scope. This chapter shows simplified European peasant costumes which are easily translated into doll dresses. For more advanced peasant and period costumes study the photographs in the next chapter, for they offer a wealth of authentic detail and design inspiration!

A JOEL ELLIS DOLL *(opposite page)*

This doll in her original clothes shows little sign of wear or neglect. Made in Vermont in 1873, she is, in a sense, a sophisticated version of the earlier New England articulated Penny Woodens. Her clothes, while nicely made, show the country-dressmaker touch of out-of-scale cutting and trimming. The metal hands and feet are characteristic of Ellis dolls.

MARY, QUEEN OF SCOTS

This exquisite doll by Dorothy Heizer is, like all her historical portrait dolls, based on a contemporary painting of the subject. Her first dolls were of the soft rag type but quickly developed into an exquisitely realistic technique perfect for portraiture. The beauty of her faces and hands is matched in the marvelous costumes Mrs. Heizer made. Frequently the fabrics are of the period of the portrait. Heizer historical portrait dolls may be seen at the Smithsonian Institution, Washington, D. C.

4.

Dolls in Foreign Dress and Historical Costumes

*T*HE DOLL DRESSMAKER AND DOLL COLLECTOR, TO SAY nothing of the teacher and educator, have a vast field of beauty and historically significant material to draw from when dealing with dolls in authentic peasant and historical dress. The average doll fancier cannot help being enchanted with the tremendous variety and extraordinary detail that individualizes the costumes of the dolls shown photographically on the following pages.

The foreign dress dolls are, for the most part, bisque. They were dressed many years ago in the countries they represent. The costumes are authentic and made of materials that duplicate the actual clothes of the peoples they represent.

These dolls are selected not only for their beauty and costume interest, but because they are defined clearly enough to allow the doll dressmaker or student to examine the important details of individual dress. Naturally, the very best way of examining such details is to see and, if possible, handle representative dolls in foreign dress that belong to some available collection.

The Children's Museum of Brooklyn, N. Y., and the Children's Museum of Detroit, Michigan (a part of the school system of that city, under the Division of Instruction), have notable and extensive doll collections that may be studied by school groups and interested adults. There are, no doubt, other museums in the country where similar study of dolls may be possible.

There are many beautifully illustrated books on the costumes of other lands available in most public libraries. The time required for study of regional and historical styles more than repays the effort involved. Aside from the point of determining the authenticity of individual details—and their importance cannot be too strongly emphasized—the many divergent avenues such study inevitably leads into are extremely alluring.

In pursuing the whys and wherefores of, say, different kinds of sleeves, the amount of information concerning various customs and cultures is automatically and entertainingly picked up. Even the most casual student acquires a keen appreciation of the social, economic and climatic background influential in the development of individual styles. Such appreciation stimulates a closer understanding of the people involved and a recognition of their problems and dreams which are not too different from our own.

Beginning on page 80 a group of 28 modern bisque dolls dressed in costumes dating in style from 1327 to 1876 is shown for period and costume design study. Many of the costumes are made from fabrics contemporary with the period they portray. All of the dolls were wigged with authentic hair-dos. To try to duplicate such exquisite costuming is neither feasible nor practical. However, the *characteristic effect* of period costumes is obtained by duplicating the silhouettes of the gowns, the headdresses and major details of styling.

In dressing all dolls, no matter what period or style, always use genuine fabrics (silk, wool, cotton, linen), not modern synthetic fibers or combinations of synthetic with genuine fibers. Old fabrics (from the attic, from auctions, from the rag-bag) handle and drape better and are easier to sew on, especially when making very small garments. Wash (or dry clean) and iron the fabrics carefully before cutting and sewing. For intricate costumes cut and fit a master pattern using cleansing tissue. Only the highly expert dressmaker can afford freehand cutting.

MARGARET OF ANJOU

Another Heizer queen portrait. Her dark green velvet gown is of fabric dating
from 1450.

HEAD-DRESS FASHIONS

Particularly noteworthy in this group is the type of head covering. From wrapped veil swathing head and throat, to the extraordinary edifice at lower right, they designate significant periods in fashion.

Upper left: Burgundian, 1420-1460

Lower left: French, 1420-1460

Lower right: English, 1327-1337

Above: English, 1536

Below: German, 1510-1540

Above: German, Nuremberg—1500-1530

Below: French, 1440-1480

Top: Dutch, 1620-1650

Lower left: French, 1660-1680

Lower right: English, 1630-1650

Top: English, 1750-1775

Lower left: French, 1661-1751

Lower right: French, 1745-1760

Top: French, 1723-1760

Lower left: French, 1774-1792

Lower right: French, 1775-1790

An 18th
Century Wooden
Doll from
England

DOLL WITH BUSTLE

The elaborate draping
towards the back of the
French style, 1872-1876.

DOLLS FROM A
FRENCH PERIOD

The French Revolution swept away
class distinction and its accompanying frivolousness of dress. Fashions
toned down until the silhouette was
more nearly normal than it had been
for over four hundred years. This
slender period was relatively short
lived.

Upper right:
French, 1807-1815

Lower right:
French, 1790-1795

Lower left:
French, 1815-1819

FRENCH AND
AMERICAN STYLES

Upper right:
    French, 1842-1847

Lower right:
    French, 1850-1858

Lower left:
    American, 1855-1862

DUTCH COUPLE
These dolls have cloth hands and arms. Girl's lace cap is particularly lovely.

DANISH BOY AND GIRL
Girl's blouse and apron are trimmed with famous Hedebo embroidery.

ITALIAN PEASANT DOLL

Handmade lace trims collar and cuffs, and gold braid borders bodice and skirt *(left)*. Dark apron has two rows of figured material and the hat shows a sweeping brim and back section.

SWISS DOLL

This doll *(right)* is dressed as a typical Swiss housewife, with woolen dress and apron. The blouse is fine muslin and over-bodice is metal trimmed. Black handmade lace forms the flowing cap.

UNUSUAL DOLLS

Right: a bisque doll dressed in Jerusalem in 1897. The costume is made of native textiles and illustrates the dress common in that period. This doll is most unusual in being about the only native dressed doll of Hebrew origin. The doll below was costumed in 1903 at a Convent in Macon, Ga. Both dolls are owned by the Doll Museum, Wenham, Mass.

BRETON FISHING COUPLE

Entirely carved of wood but dressed in fabrics. The girl's china head is a replacement of the original wooden one. The man's face is particularly fine.

AN IRISH PAIR

Both complete with hand knit stockings. The girl's hooded cape is worn over a white linen bonnet, typical of late 19th century dress.

MEXICAN AND CUBAN DOLLS

Our Latin neighbors have developed distinctive styles in dolls designed to catch the tourist's eye. The Mexican woman has been "prettied" for better sales appeal. There is a sly and attractive sense of humor in the Cuban dancer, a quality which occurs in most of the dolls from that island.

A CHINESE MAN AND WIFE

These dolls are authentically costumed in heavy silk damask. The man's short jacket is
worn over a full-length robe which buttons to right side in the same way as his wife's.

A particularly fine example of both carving and costuming, the Eskimo figures below are of interest to the student of racial and national dress. The dark smudge on the mother's chin is a tatoo mark.

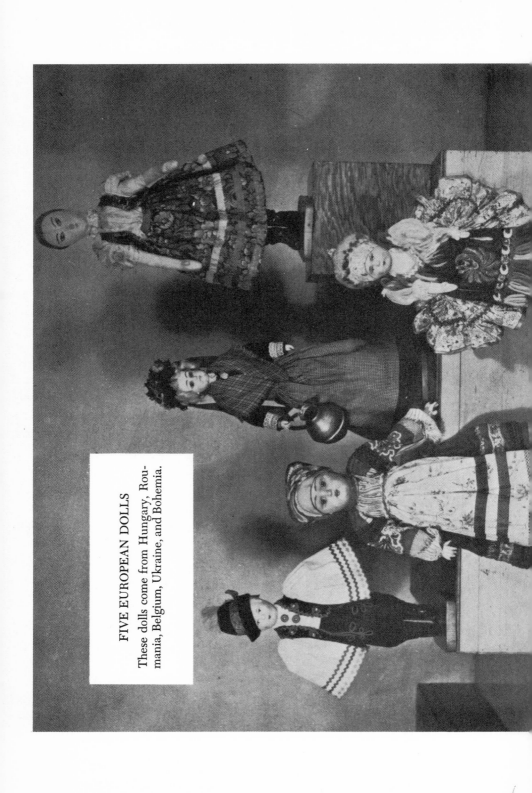

FIVE EUROPEAN DOLLS

These dolls come from Hungary, Roumania, Belgium, Ukraine, and Bohemia.

LENCI'S LITTLE PEASANT GIRL

Her simplified costume is capable of many detail changes that can transform her nationality. Remove head scarf and wooden shoes, put on a white ruffled pinafore and she becomes an American or English schoolgirl of the 1870's. Or, an embroidered black sateen apron, shoulder shawl and a flat-brimmed black felt hat and she'll become a Central European girl. Try your own changes.

THE FISH BASKET WEAVER

Created by Jeanne Maker of Maine, this salty character is one of a series of Down East fishermen. Pure Americana, they are a pure delight to examine. The fidelity of detailing and perfect scaling of accessories and amounts contributes largely to their personality and the gentle humor with which they are portrayed. Made of padded wire frames covered with jersey, each figure is dressed authentically. Faces are molded to achieve effect rather than as literal representations of features. Mouth and eyes are embroidered. Since each one is an original, not too many of them are around. Some have found their way into museums. They're worth searching out to examine and enjoy.

Dorothy Heizer created her dolls from 1921 to 1961, specializing in historical portrait dolls. However, she made many other dolls with the same artistry and meticulous attention to the designing and execution of their costumes. The two beauties shown here represent the periods of 1900 and 1925.

5.

Making Novelty Dolls for Fun and Entertainment

THE LIST OF UNUSUAL MATERIALS WITH WHICH TO MAKE dolls and figures is practically limitless. Human ingenuity, fired by a creative instinct, has produced an amazing array of exhibits. Some have been made with the completely serious intent of "making a doll for Mary," others as humorous whimsies.

Lack of money or the proper materials has seldom stopped the amateur doll maker when the happiness of the daughter of the house depended upon producing a doll baby for her enjoyment. All that is needed is a little imagination forced into action by the pressure of the child's desires. Many a wooden potato masher has vanished from the kitchen to reappear disguised and dressed as the latest member of the doll family. The use of corn husks with which to make dolls is extremely well known, as is the stringing together of peanuts, wooden spools, corks, acorns and dried seed pods, etc.

SOUTHERN MAMMY AND BABY

Black rubber old-fashioned nursing nipples, stuffed with cotton

POTATO
MASHER
DOLL

MAMMY
AND BABY
MADE FROM
NIPPLE

and having painted features, make very acceptable heads for small Mammy dolls. Tie a bit of colored rag around the head and cement the nipple to a plump wad of cotton batting. Dress in the simplest of dresses, and you have a real southern Mammy to put into the doll nursery. Her baby? That's even simpler. A piece of linen about 6 inches long and 2 inches wide is folded in half, lengthwise, and rolled up. Penciled features, a wee bit of lace sewn into a cap and an equally wee "kimono" dress with the arms stuffed with bits of cotton and the baby is ready for her Mammy's arms.

YARN DOLLS

Left-over knitting yarn can be turned into delightful dolls with a minimum of effort. Make a thick hank of yarn by winding it around a piece of cardboard that is 5 or 6 inches long. Tie one end of the hank together at the top, then slip out the cardboard. About 1 inch below top, tie-wrap the hank tightly with matching yarn to make the neck. Cut the bottom of the hank. Separate the strands in half and slip a shorter and thinner hank between them, placing it directly below the neck wrapping. This makes the arms, and the hands are indicated by wrapping the ends of this hank a little dis-

Left: Corncob doll with floss hair and cotton stuffed arms.

Below: Pipestem cleaner frame dipped several times in ivory-colored wax (melted candle). Yarn hair is pushed into scalp while wax is soft. This 2-inch doll is dressed in very soft muslin.

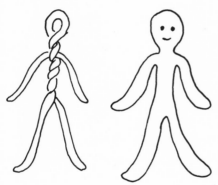

tance in to form wrists. Wrap the waistline tightly. To make legs, divide the lower strands in half and wrap them near the bottom to form ankles. Girl dolls need no legs as the strands of yarn may be considered a skirt.

How to Dress Up the Yarn Doll. As it is, the yarn doll is rather amusing. It can be made more so by adding a few accessories such as a kerchief tied on the head, a gay bit of material made into a tiny apron, even a whole dress or suit made of colorful scraps of material. These "fashion" accessories may also be crocheted. Add a perky cap or felt hat trimmed with a bird's feather and you have

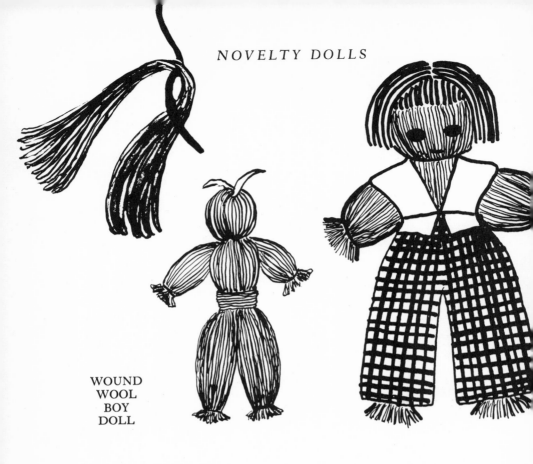

WOUND
WOOL
BOY
DOLL

a dashing creation which has been as much fun to create as almost anything else you could do in an hour or two.

SEA SHELLS

It has always been the popular and obvious thing to make jewelry out of the lovely little sea shells that may be picked up at the beach. Often you may overlook larger shells in the search for tiny beauties. Yet these larger ones offer tremendous opportunities for making imaginative doll figures. The photos on page 105 illustrate how Mrs. Florence Bradshaw Brown transformed quite common and ordinary sea shells into fabulous creatures that enchanted her grandchildren (and everyone else who saw them). A hand drill, some fine copper wire and cement, activated by a sense of humor and imagination, will produce shell dolls of distinctive personalities and appeal.

THE SHELL FAMILY

Created by Florence Bradshaw Brown, these entertaining shell figures are a perfect illustration of the possibilities inherent in very simple materials.

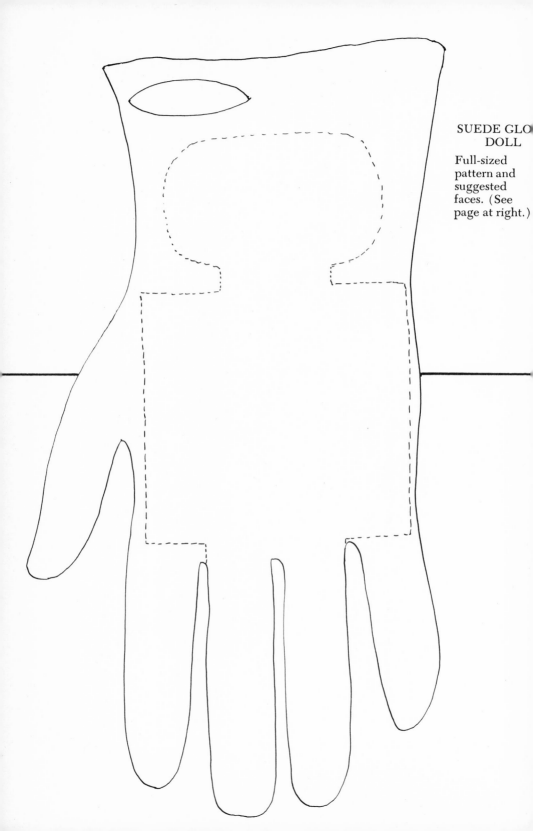

SUEDE GLOVE
DOLL

Full-sized
pattern and
suggested
faces. (See
page at right.)

EAST INDIAN
DOLLS WITH
SUEDE BODIES

CHAMOIS SKINS AND OLD GLOVES

You may take an old suede or kidskin glove or an ordinary piece of chamois skin and devise a dusky-skinned doll. Which would you prefer—an Indian brave or a squaw and papoose? Use the fingers of the glove for arms and legs, a piece of the palm for the head. Attach these, after stuffing, to a simple cloth body, or even tack them to a piece of wood of a size and shape to approximate a body. The chamois makes wonderful "buckskins." Sew a few small bright beads to add to the effectiveness and, of course, tiny slashings along the lower edges of the garments complete the picture. The same body technique may be used for Eskimos, Laplanders, Arabs and other dark-skinned races whose costumes are loosely enveloping.

SOAP HEADS

You may carve very good looking doll shoulder-heads from your toilet or laundry soap. The easiest way is to carve the head and body in one piece, following the general pattern of the Penny Wooden doll design on page 128. With a kitchen paring knife, block out the main areas, then slowly and carefully, proceed with the finer cutting. Soap is so soft in comparison with wood that practically no strength is needed in cutting. When you are satisfied with the shape, you finish the surface by delicately scraping it with the knife blade held at right angles to the soap. If the results do not please you, the whole thing can go into the washing machine.

Painting soap is not difficult. Use poster paint or opaque water colors. Either should be very thin and brushed on quickly. Too heavy a coat of paint destroys the translucent quality of the soap.

Putting Wigs on the Soap Head. Short curly hair goes on rather easily. If you use long hair, it is better to make it in a wig form and then paste it to the soap skull with sodium silicate. To make short curls, ravel out a piece of knitting yarn of a color that looks like hair. Cut the yarn into short pieces. These are pushed into the head, piece by piece, with a tapestry needle which has had half the eye end cut off. The yarn is held by the "prong" of the needle which slips out easily, leaving the wool in the head. Press the hole

TWO WAY DOLL

Cut body pattern as shown. Two pieces, front and back, are joined with a half-inch bias strip around both sides and over each head. Embroider or paint on features. Cut eight arm pieces, (two pieces needed for each arm) sew together and stuff, then sew to shoulders. Make bodices and sew on to top of each doll, having the waistlines meet and sewn down flat to body. The skirts are straight strips of material sewn together along the lower edge, turned inside out and pressed. Shirr top edge of the reversible skirt. Fit snugly to body of doll and sew down securely. Rough seam line is concealed by wide sash on Little Eva side of doll. Mammy's apron is sewed on.

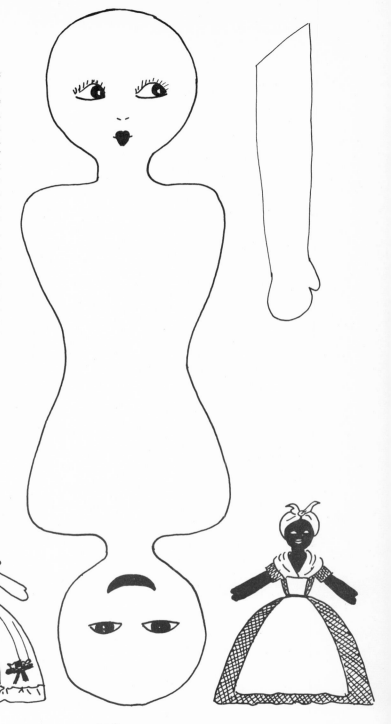

109

closed before inserting the next piece. Do not try to set the yarn pieces too close together. After cutting to desired length, the ends may be fluffed out gently to completely cover the scalp.

Using a Body of Soap. If you carve a body of soap for your doll, cover it with a form-fitting piece of muslin and sew on the kind of arms and legs you choose. If the soap doll is actually destined for a plaything force a metal meat skewer up through the body, neck and head. Do this carefully, starting it at a point which will bring the skewer directly through the center of the neck. The moisture in the soap will rust the metal skewer thus holding it in permanently.

Give soap a coat of clear lacquer to preserve it. White soap will, in time, acquire a delicate ivory color that is quite beautiful. If really good carving is done it is worth while to put the finished work aside for several months to allow this ivory tone to develop. Then lacquer it.

DRIED FRUIT FACES

Almost as long as people have been growing apples and pears, they have used the fruit for dolls' heads. Both fruits shrink and go brown in drying. A little preliminary carving before the drying process results in interesting faces usually associated with really old peasants. For generations, the carvers of France and Switzerland have made dolls this way.

Select under-ripe fruit that is normally firm and crisp of flesh. Peel and thrust a wooden skewer up into the bottom, leaving enough projecting below head to make a neck. With a penknife carve a quite bold nose. Scoop out shallow eye sockets and indicate the mouth with a moderately deep slash. Carve away below the chin. The profile should be bold and well defined. The natural shrinkage which takes place will diminish the size of the features considerably. Push a small-headed clove into each eye socket, embedding it quite deeply. These are the eyeballs and are later touched with a dot of white paint to give them brilliance and sparkle.

The carved fruit must be dehydrated in a place that is free of drafts and quite dry; otherwise, it will get moldy. A few experiments will indicate how much preliminary carving is required to

APPLES AND PEARS

Top and middle photos show dried pears transformed into amusing and well detailed dolls by Anne Davis. It is that careful attention to details which makes them distinctive. Doll at right is from Switzerland having a dried apple head.

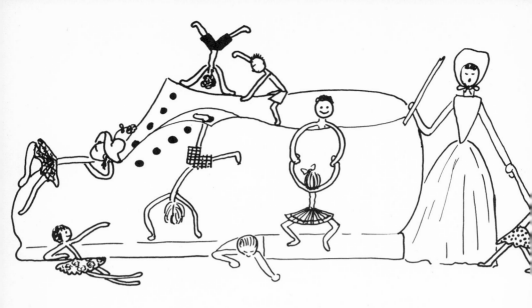

PIPE STEM CLEANER PARTY PIECE ... OLD WOMAN WHO LIVED IN SHOE

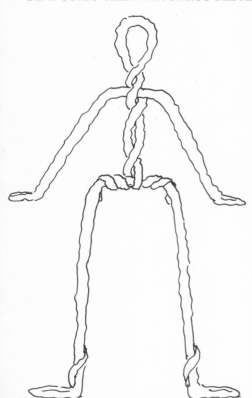

The construction of these amusing little pipe stem cleaner dolls is shown on the opposite page. The small figures are made from two cleaners, the larger figures from three or more cleaners. The dolls illustrated above have heads made from small lumps of putty or crack filler (moistened to proper workable consistency) pressed around head-loop. They are allowed to dry before features are put on with India ink. Hair is small bits of wool cemented on. The clothes are made from gay scraps of paper cemented to the dolls. The girls' skirts are half circles. Bend the dolls into the desired poses before cementing on the skirts or shorts. The Old Woman is dressed in crepe paper. The skirt is gathered at the waist, the bodice is two flat pieces cemented on after skirt has been adjusted.

On the following pages are six other pipe stem cleaner dolls which are dressed in nursery rhyme character costumes. The heads of these dolls may be of crack filler, or putty or of wads of cotton covered with fine cloth. The bodies are not wrapped unless desired. Clothes of paper (crepe or cleansing tissue), are easily made and cemented on. While quite attractive in their paper costumes, the use of supple, semi-sheer woven fabrics offers

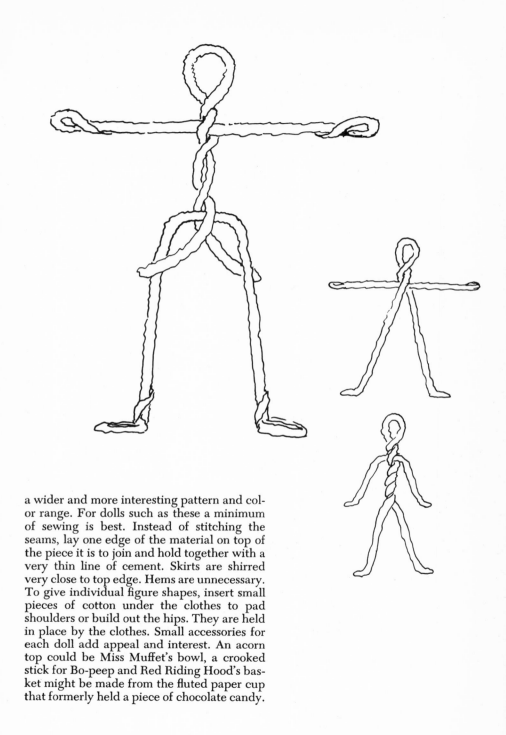

a wider and more interesting pattern and color range. For dolls such as these a minimum of sewing is best. Instead of stitching the seams, lay one edge of the material on top of the piece it is to join and hold together with a very thin line of cement. Skirts are shirred very close to top edge. Hems are unnecessary. To give individual figure shapes, insert small pieces of cotton under the clothes to pad shoulders or build out the hips. They are held in place by the clothes. Small accessories for each doll add appeal and interest. An acorn top could be Miss Muffet's bowl, a crooked stick for Bo-peep and Red Riding Hood's basket might be made from the fluted paper cup that formerly held a piece of chocolate candy.

Left:
RED RIDING HOOD

Below:
BO-PEEP

Right:
GOLDILOCKS

Left:
BAHAMIAN BEAUTY

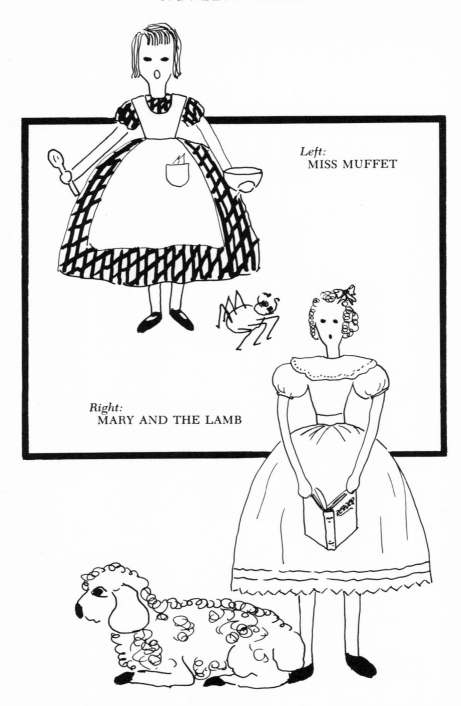

Left:
MISS MUFFET

Right:
MARY AND THE LAMB

get certain results. Wrinkles, which occur naturally in the drying, may be emphasized and directed by scoring the fruit with the fingernail or knifepoint along the desired lines.

Finish the face with a touch of color high on the cheeks and lips. Sometimes the entire face is painted with a base coat before the features are colored. A more interesting effect is obtained by simply coloring the features, then lacquering the entire head. Attach wool hair and tiny eyebrows while the lacquer is still wet.

CLOTHESPIN DOLLS

You may make attractive little doll-house dolls and party favors from ordinary clothespins. The slit of the pin should face you as you place a wad of cotton over the top and cover it with a piece of thin muslin or cotton jersey. Hold this tight by wrapping thread around the indentation at the top of the clothespin. Tiny clothes are made as desired, stuffing the sleeves slightly with cotton to make arms. A pipe stem cleaner inserted in the sleeve makes it possible to bend the arms into natural positions. The clothespin doll may be made to stand by itself by setting the ends into small wads of self-hardening clay and allowing it to dry in an upright

BOY AND GIRL CLOTHESPIN DOLLS

MARY ANN and the SOLDIER BOY

These are cunning little dolls that are easily made. Being extremely lightweight, they make good toys for young children. Their secret is the ping pong ball used for the head. While I made them with a pair of infant's socks, practically any other type of fabric may be used for the bodies. The virtue of the sock lies in the fact that it can be drawn down smoothly over the ball and the rest of the sock is just the right size and shape for making the body and legs. They may be dressed in any number of ways lending themselves to all sorts of roles. Nursery rhyme characters are particularly appropriate for this style of doll for it has a directness and simplicity that young children find very appealing.

position. Indicate features with paint or thin pointed crayon pencils or embroidery stitches.

RUBBER BALL HEADS

You may use lightweight rubber balls for doll heads in much the same way as the ping pong dolls shown on page 118, or the ball head may be left uncovered. In either case, make a slit on the bottom of the ball about one-quarter inch long. Through this slit force a half-inch wooden dowel that is long enough to reach to the inside top of the head and to protrude below about two inches. Nail a carpet tack through the rubber into the top of the dowel.

A Body for the Rubber Ball. While it is easier to cover the head with the same piece of material that makes the body (a sock, for instance), an uncovered head with painted complexion and features makes an interesting change in style. You will need a crosspiece not only to make the shoulders, but to form a support over which the body is attached. Drill a small hole through the large dowel about one inch below the bottom of the ball head. Through this hole insert a small wooden dowel that has been cut to the desired length to approximate the width of the shoulders. An ordinary but headless stuffed fabric body can be attached to this crosspiece. Pad the top of the shoulders before sewing up the fabric.

OLD AND NEW NOVELTY DOLLS

The pages of this chapter show some of the interesting novelty dolls that have been created within the last hundred years. As curiosities, they have found their way into various doll collections. Included with them in both sketch and photographic form are a number of interesting doll novelties that are easily duplicated. Created from odd materials usually found around the house, they make delightful impromptu gifts, party favors, surprises for a sick child. All of them offer opportunity for considerable expansion and elaboration of original ideas. It is quite possible to turn these ideas into little masterpieces of skillful and imaginative workmanship. Most of them are simple enough for children to make, a few require real skill and patience. The instructions that accompany them are basic and subject to your own interpretation which, after all, increases the fun of making and improving upon the original models.

MARY ANN AND THE SOLDIER BOY

One of a pair of infant's socks, size 4, a ping pong ball and stuffing (which may be of absorbent cotton, cotton flock, crumpled tissue paper, sheared lamb's wool or raveled out knitting wools) is all you need to make these two unusual dolls.

Mary Ann. Insert a ping pong ball into the toe of a sock. Draw the sock down tightly and smoothly around the ball. Wrap thread around sock underneath ball to hold it in place and to form the neck. Use strong thread, wrapping it around ten or twelve times and tying it securely. Stuff sock, not too tightly, as far down as ribbing. Seam across at this point. The heel of the sock should not be stuffed. Fold it down flatly and slip-stitch it to "chest."

At the center of the ribbed cuff, make a vertical slit up from edge of sock to the horizontal line of stitching, cutting both back and front of the ribbing at the same time. Overcast the cut edges closely and securely. Stuff each "leg." Overcast bottom of leg, and at about one-quarter of an inch up from bottom, make "ankle" by wrapping thread around tightly. Tie and break off thread.

Mary Ann's arms are made from the ribbing of the other sock. Cut two pieces, the ribs running lengthwise, each about three-quarters of an inch wide. Overcast long edges together and around one short edge. Stuff to within half an inch of top. Make wrist like the ankle. Turn in raw top edge and lay on top of shoulder. Slip-stitch across shoulder and down each side of "arm" not more than one-quarter inch.

Mary Ann's wig can be easily put on as shown in the sketch on page 121. Her features may be painted on with textile paints or drawn on with colored pencils.

The Soldier Boy. The soldier boy needs a few additional working materials. This doll is made from the second sock, and requires legs. Most of the ribbing has been cut away to make Mary Ann's arms. Cut off the remaining ribbed piece. Put ping pong ball into

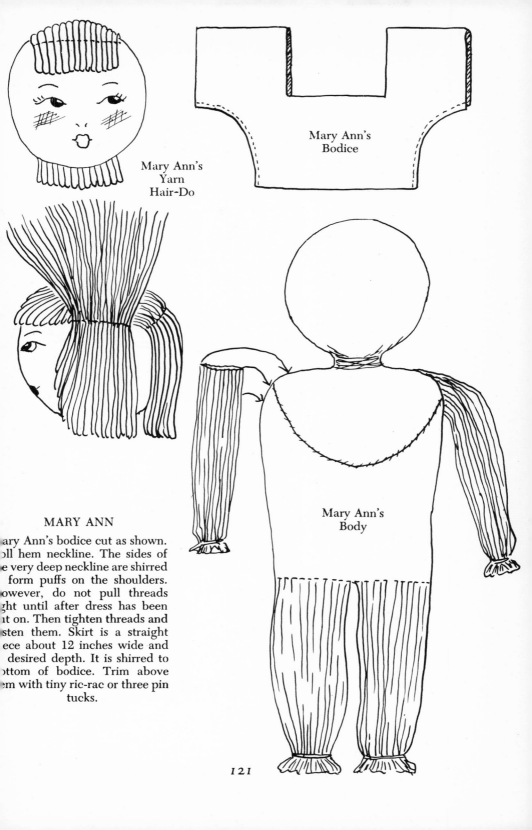

Mary Ann's
Yarn
Hair-Do

Mary Ann's
Bodice

Mary Ann's
Body

MARY ANN

ary Ann's bodice cut as shown.
oll hem neckline. The sides of
e very deep neckline are shirred
form puffs on the shoulders.
owever, do not pull threads
ght until after dress has been
it on. Then tighten threads and
sten them. Skirt is a straight
ece about 12 inches wide and
desired depth. It is shirred to
ottom of bodice. Trim above
m with tiny ric-rac or three pin
tucks.

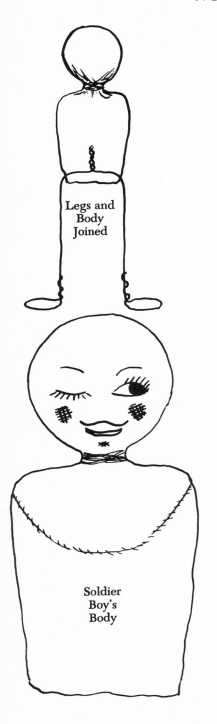

Legs and Body Joined

Soldier Boy's Body

SOLDIER BOY

Ping pong ball stuffed into toe of infant's sock which is tied tightly beneath ball to make neck. Stuff body with cotton, allowing heel of sock to fall flat on chest. Slip-stitch down. Cut off ribbing. Sew bottom.

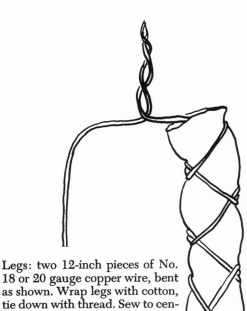

Legs: two 12-inch pieces of No. 18 or 20 gauge copper wire, bent as shown. Wrap legs with cotton, tie down with thread. Sew to center back of doll, as shown. Overcast as shown. Self-hardening clay is molded over foot loops and allowed to dry. Paint on features.

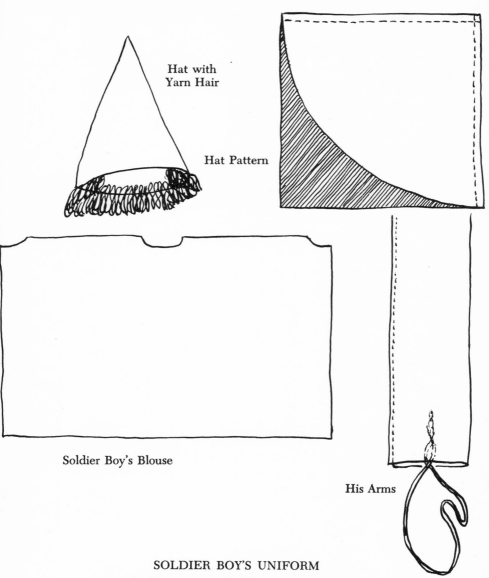

Hat with Yarn Hair

Hat Pattern

Soldier Boy's Blouse

His Arms

SOLDIER BOY'S UNIFORM

The blouse is cut double with fold at the shoulder line, seams coming under the arms. Front of blouse may have buttons and braid trimming. Sleeves are tubes of material. The hair is yarn of any color desired, and is sewed under the edge of the hat. Trim after yarn is sewed in place.

tɔe and proceed as for Mary Ann. Overcast the bottom edges together. This makes the boy's torso.

Cut two pieces of No. 18 or No. 20 gauge copper wire into 10-
inch lengths. Bend as shown in sketch and sew firmly to lower
back of boy. Wind strips of absorbent cotton or cotton batting
around legs to "flesh" them. The cotton is held on by winding
thread around it, then taking a few catch stitches at hips.

Pattern for the boy's suit is given on page 123 . Notice that his
arms are really stuffed sleeves with a wire hand sewed into the
bottom of each. The hand may be covered with adhesive tape or
mittens cut and sewed to fit. For the latter, use a knit cotton fabric
such as is found in infants' nightgowns or wrappers.

The boy's feet are simple lumps of self-hardening clay which
have been pressed down over the wire loops. The clay dries hard
and forms a very steady base for the boy to stand on. They may be
left a natural color or painted.

WOUND WIRE DOLL

Samantha is 8½ inches tall. Her body, arms and legs are a
frame of copper wire similar to the one shown on page 38. Plastic
wood was used for her hands, feet and head. Slight indentations
were made for eyes and mouth; this increases the effect of the
nose. After the plastic wood was dry, in about 24 hours, the
features were painted on and arms, legs and body were tightly
wound with cotton rug yarn. The author exaggerated her slim-
ness, which is often desirable, to increase effect of quaintness in
dressing. She was given a pair of lace ruffled organdie panties
and a simple printed cotton dress trimmed with baby ric-rac. Hair
is rug yarn, glued on strand by strand.

A styrofoam ball covered with nylon hose may be used instead
of plastic wood for the head. This speeds up the making of the
doll, thus making it an excellent item for a church bazaar.

Character and personality in homemade dolls come not only
from the face and costume you give them but also from the accessories you choose to go with them. Tiny artificial flowers, a tiny
toy or musical instrument, or a small Mexican basket such as
Samantha is carrying, contribute considerably to their effective-

SAMANTHA, THE WOUND WIRE DOLL

Tiny Penny Wooden dolls in the clothes their young owner made in 1838 after buying them in the Cent Shop in the House of the Seven Gables, Salem, Mass. They came down in her family until presented to the author in 1947.

ness. Always be sure such items are in scale with the size of the doll.

WHITTLE A WOODEN DOLL

Whittling skill is no masculine prerogative. Any hands that have pared potatoes or apples, diced vegetables or had experience in any of the many forms of "cutting" required to make a meal, have all the required dexterity and strength for whittling out wooden dolls. These dolls are fascinating to make and are, perhaps, the most versatile of all dolls for costuming.

The diagrams given on page 128 are based on the old Penny Woodens so popular in the last century. Don't be alarmed at the apparent complexity of the diagram. It probably seems so because, unlike your husband or brother, you are unused to reading such diagrams. This one will produce a doll about 9½ inches tall.

The Tools Are Simple. While the whittling may be done with an ordinary sharp penknife, it will be very much easier to work with an X-acto knife. A hand drill is necessary for the holes in the legs and arms through which the joint pegs are inserted. A jigsaw is a help in sawing off large chunks of wood unnecessary to the shaping of the doll. These chunks, of course, may be whittled off if you insist but it is much faster to saw them off.

White pine, poplar, willow or holly wood may be used for the body and head which are carved out in one piece. The legs and arms are wooden dowels obtained from a lumber mill or hobby shop. The pegs for jointing may either be very thin wooden dowels or, as I have used, short pieces of kitchen matches.

The block from which the head and torso are to be shaped should be 4¾ inches long, 1½ inches wide and 1¼ inches thick. Since these are not standard wood measurements, it will be necessary to saw the wood to size. When doing so, be sure that all corners are truly squared, i.e., at perfect right angles to each other.

Trace Your Design. Make a tracing of both the side, front and back views of the doll and transfer them to the sides, front and back of the block of wood. Be sure to mark on the block the little circles indicated at the shoulder and hip line of the doll. Bore a hole through these circles, from side to side, making the upper one with a quarter-inch drill, the lower with an eighth-inch drill. The pegs holding the arms and legs are later run through these drill holes. Notice that just below the shoulder line in back there are two drill holes indicated. Made with an eighth-inch drill, these go into torso about a half-inch. They should cut through the lower part of the transverse hold. They are necessary for securing the shoulder pegs to keep them from slipping out. Saw off the unnecessary pieces as indicated by the dotted lines on the diagram.

Keep Turning as You Whittle. Now, actual whittling begins. Carve out the torso first, turning it as you work rather than concentrating on one side. Keep the diagram near you for reference so that the required measurements are adhered to. When the body is fairly well shaped up, start blocking out the head, keeping the sides and back quite round in silhouette. The face, as indicated in the profile sketch, is worked out to a definite point which forms the nose.

The shoulder and breast line is indicated by the curved lines on

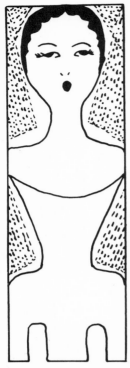

A MODERN PENNY WOODEN DOLL

Trace outlines on block of wood. Then carve down to outline as shown. Measurements and full instructions on page 126. *(Below)* Pieces are cut from wood dowels. A. Front view of lower leg. B. Side view of lower leg. C. Front view of upper leg. The tongue at top fits into groove at bottom of body. D. Front view of upper arm. E. Front view of lower arm. F. Transverse hold which fits through shoulder. Tongue with small hole extends outside of shoulder for pegging upper arm. Cut two pieces of each of A, B, C, D, E. F. Lower legs and arms from wood dowels as A and E. Upper legs and arms of cloth. G and H wood parts are slipped inside as indicated by dotted lines, wrapped with cord at small end, then cloth is turned right side and stuffed. Tack to wood body.

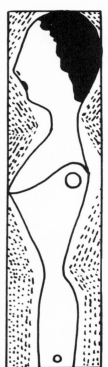

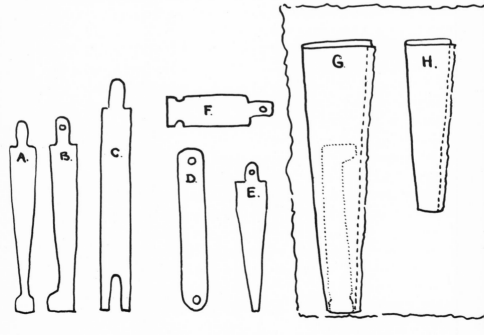

the front and side views. All carving done above should be lightly and finely stroked. The carving below the shoulder-breast line may be done with heavier and sharper slashes that tend to flatten the torso. They, of course, are done much more quickly. The waistline must be quite narrow and thin.

Short Strokes for Graceful Curves. When working reverse curves such as those that mark the chest, throat and chin line it is easier to carve a few short strokes, then turn the work upside down and carve additional strokes to meet the first ones. This way you achieve a smoother and more graceful curve. The line from the shoulder down to the waist and out to curve the pelvis is worked the same way.

Help Yourself in Father's Workshop. After completing the head and torso, saw notches in the lower part to correspond with the notches in the diagram. These are for attaching the legs. They should be five-eighths inch deep and about three-eighths wide. Hold the torso in a vise while sawing, otherwise the cuts will be uneven. If your husband's workshop has a very small rounded chisel, use it to cut out the notch after the sawcuts have been made. Otherwise, make a series of parallel cuts with the jigsaw as indicated by the dotted lines on the sketch. The knife is then used to cut out these slivers, leaving a notch of the necessary width and depth.

Sandpaper the head, neck and shoulders to remove all knife marks. Paint this part of the doll with white enamel and let dry while making the arms and legs.

Using three-eighth inch dowels, cut two pieces each 3 inches long for the upper legs; two pieces 2½ inches long for the lower legs; two pieces 2¼ inches long for the upper arms; two pieces 2 inches long for the lower arms. Drill holes as indicated in the sketch, then saw the ends of the dowels as shown. The lower arms are whittled down to form a blunt point at the end. Whittle the lower leg as shown to indicate a foot. Paint lower legs and lower arms with white enamel. When dry, paint on tiny black or red slippers.

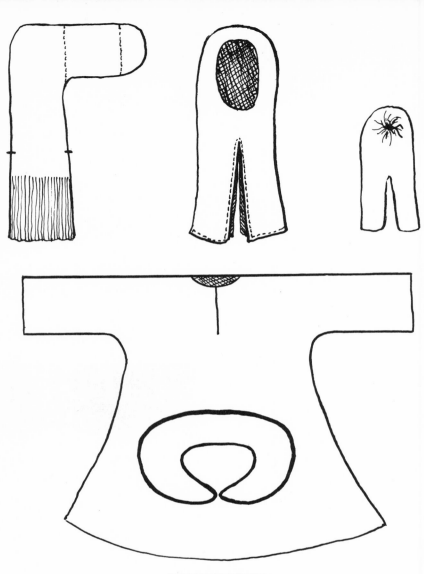

HOW TO MAKE
SLEEPY SOCKO

A white sock is laid flat as shown. The foot is cut off along the dotted line and put aside. The leg part of sock is slashed up each side to marks just above ribbing. Now pick up cut sock and fold so that leg slashes are centered with opening above that has been formed by removing foot of sock. Sew legs together as shown. Stuff doll's legs and body through large opening. Stuff head and then draw edges of opening together with tight firm stitches. Wrap thread tightly around neck and make secure. The arms are cut from foot of sock after toe has been cut off. Sew arm pieces together, stuff and sew to shoulders. Socko's features may be painted or embroidered on. Make eyes, then sew tiny half-circle eyelids over the eyes. Blonde curls are made of pale yellow zephyr wool

which has been dampened, wound around a small knitting needle and allowed to dry. Snip into short lengths and tack to head. Socko's nightgown is cut as shown having fold of material across top of shoulder. Use sheer batiste or lawn. A wee lace edging to collar is very dainty and well worth the trouble of putting on. To complete the picture, make a ruffled pillow of matching lawn or batiste.

131

Kitchen Matches for Pegs. Use kitchen matches or very thin wood dowels to peg the limbs together. Fit the tenons into the proper joints. It may be necessary to pare them a bit so that they will move easily. Be sure, however, not to pare off too much. The tenon should fit the joint snugly enough to remain in position. Gently force the pegs through the holes and trim off any projections.

Painting the Features. Before fitting the limbs to the torso, finish painting it. The head and shoulders may need a second coat of white. When dry, paint the hair with black enamel. A red oval indicates the mouth, two tiny red dots are nostrils. With a thin pointed brush put on the brows and upper lids with black paint. Delicately indicate eyelashes as shown in the sketch on page 128. Paint the eyes the desired color, blue, green or brown. Now, the limbs may be pegged to the torso. The peg for the legs should be exactly the width of the hips. Trim off any projections.

The shoulder pegs are somewhat different from the others. Cut two pieces, 1⅛ inch long, from quarter-inch dowel. Shape them as shown in the sketch. Insert each peg into shoulder holes so that the "waisted" ends almost meet in center of shoulders. The "waists" should come just where the small drill holes go through. Put small pegs into the back drill holes. Tap them until they go in all the way, then trim off the projections. These pegs allow each arm to be worked forward or backward, independently of each other. Attach upper arms to shoulder pegs as indicated.

Now, you have a real Penny Wooden.

If You Want an Easier Penny Wooden. If you want to get the effect of a Penny Wooden without bothering with all the drilling and notching and cutting of the arms and legs, it can be done as follows:

Make and paint the torso as explained, eliminating the drill holes. Cut from wooden dowels the lower arms and legs only. At the top of each arm and leg piece cut a narrow channel as shown on page 128. Carve the feet and hands. Paint them.

From muslin or other firm material, cut pieces according to the patterns in G and H. These make the upper arms and legs. Do not turn them inside out yet. Slip the wooden leg down the tube so that the upper part meets the narrow end of the cloth tube. Wrap strong thread around both cloth and wood, pulling the thread tightly into the channel of the wood. Tie securely. Now slip the cloth tube down so it automatically turns inside out. Stuff almost to top. Tack to sides of lower torso. The same procedure is followed for the other leg and both arms. Take care that all seams of the cloth tubes are so placed that they run along the backs of the arms and legs.

That's all there is to it.

CHINA BOY

The composition China Boy, page 134, was made in Germany and dressed in China during the early 1920's. His soft body is stuffed with cotton.

Making the Jacket. The solid black line indicates the outline of the jacket. While it may be cut in one piece, as shown, it is more authentic to have a center seam down the center back. It is cut from doubled material, the fold line of which makes the top of the sleeves. The side seams are stitched from the bottom of the sleeves to the circle on each side. From that point, the sides of the jacket are left open. Neck is finished with a narrow, straight piece, forming the collar.

The dotted line indicates the extra piece of the front which allows the jacket to be buttoned far over on the right side. This piece is seamed to left front center.

The piece with the pinked edges is cut from doubled material to form the trousers. Two pieces are necessary.

The Value of Lining. In the original, both the jacket and trousers are fully lined with lightweight muslin. This is the best way to make these garments, as the lining makes them hang with a characteristic stiffness and preciseness. The lining is cut exactly the same as the outer parts. Very narrow black braid is used to make the three tiny buttons and frogged loops.

The slippers may be cut from black felt which eliminates hemming or turning in. Put a few stitches of bright thread embroidery on their tips.

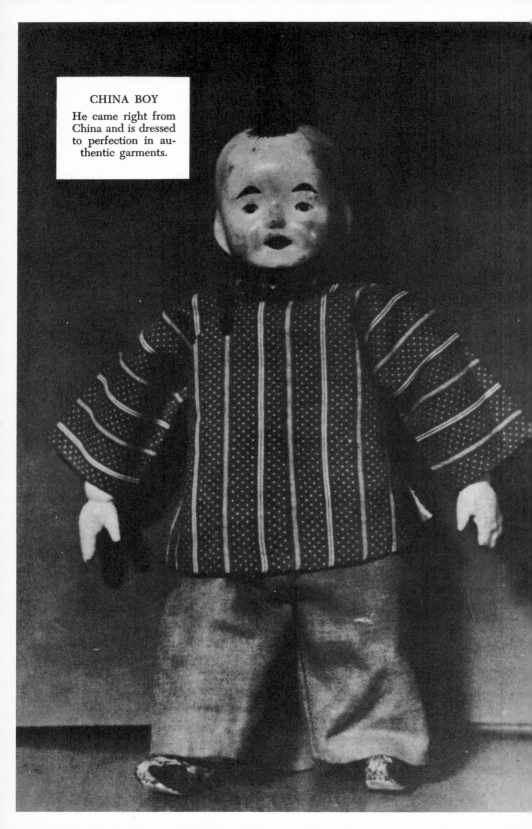

CHINA BOY

He came right from China and is dressed to perfection in authentic garments.

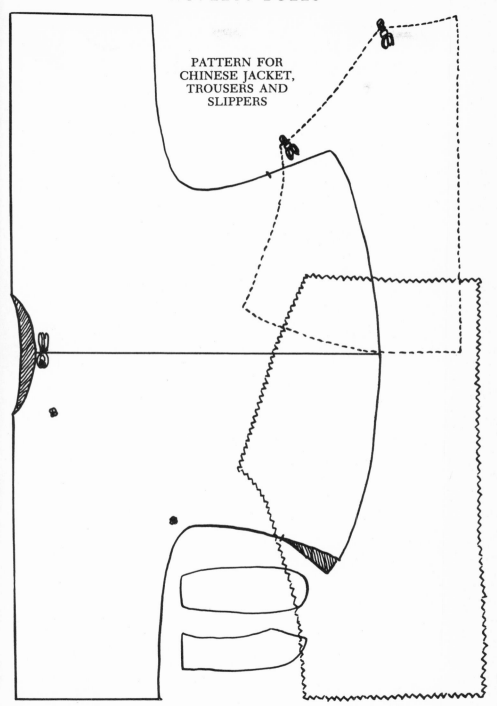

PATTERN FOR
CHINESE JACKET,
TROUSERS AND
SLIPPERS

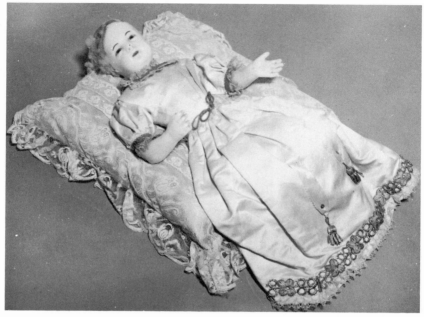

POURED WAX BABY DOLL

This doll, elaborately gowned in silk satin, and resting on a lace-covered satin pillow, is probably English. Late 19th century. 17 inches tall.

6.

How to Model and Cast Doll Heads

*I*T CAN BE DONE, AND RATHER CREDIBLY TOO, EVEN IF you have had little or no experience in working with modeling clay and taking casts. There are tricks to this, as to every other trade. One of the main things to keep in mind is the fact that you are not trying to create a piece of *art* but are attempting to depict a reasonable facsimile of the human face and head. The secret lies in the phrase "reasonable facsimile."

Use professional sculptors' clay, having an oil base so it may be used over and over again. Five pounds of it will be ample. Break medium sized pieces from the clay and work them together in the palm of the hand. Keep adding to this ball until it is of such size as desired. The easiest size to start with is an oval form about the size and shape of a duck's egg. The pointed end of the oval is the chin, the rounded end the crown of the head.

Holding the egg at an angle, start adding clay to form the neck and shoulders. Always make additions of clay with small pieces and press them firmly to the larger mass. Your eye will tell you when the length of the neck looks right. Start building it out to make the shoulders which should be only slightly wider than the greatest width of the head. Carry the shoulders down almost to the breast line.

While building up this basic form do not waste time by trying to keep it smooth. That comes later. Up to this point the main effort is towards forming a mass that, in proportion and outline, approximates a bald skull on a strong, well poised neck and shoulder base.

MODELING THE FEATURES

This is where the "reasonable facsimile" part comes in. The idea is to suggest rather than to detail exactly every curve and indentation of the human face. Look at a child's face. The cheeks are plump and definitely curved outward. The forehead curves outward. The nose is really a charming little lump with more exaggerated curves. It, too, curves outward. The chin is another, somewhat larger, lump that curves out. The valleys between these various hills are shallow and merge gracefully and meltingly into the higher parts.

These characteristic hills or lumps are *added* to the egg shape, not carved out from it. With tiny bits of clay, build them up rather higher than you think they should be for the necessary smoothing that comes later will pare off some of their bulk and height.

Before starting to build up the features study the sketches on page 21. The natural impulse is to place the features much higher on the face than they should be. Notice that, especially in a very young child's face, all of the features are placed almost entirely on the lower half of the egg. The eyebrows actually come at about the midpoint between the crown and the tip of the chin. To restrain your impulse to set the features higher, draw a line right across the egg halfway between the top of the head and the tip of the chin. Leave that line there until all the main features have been added.

Start With the Nose. Roll a small bit of clay between the thumb and forefinger into a flattish ball shape. Press it firmly in the direct center between the drawn line and tip of chin. With other small pieces, build up each cheek. Place a small flat lump on tip of chin. Build out the forehead, directly above the drawn line, with thin flat

MODELING MATERIALS

These consist mainly of clay, one or two tools, wire and your own fingers. The head arma-ture (wire frame on stick shown above) is not necessary for doll heads but is useful because you may save clay by stuffing center of wire frame with crumpled newspaper and then building clay around it. Without an armature one simply builds the clay, in an egg shape, on the end of a stick long enough to be held in the hand while working on it. Use the best grade clay you can get, it models easier.

pieces of clay. It is a lumpy looking piece of work by now but should have a very definite, if quite rough, resemblance to a face.

All this building up naturally forms the concave areas where the eyes are to set. Do not try to model the eye forms as professional sculptors do. Simply see that the cavities are not too deep and are approximately the size of the desired eye socket. Keep them widely spaced, allowing a little more distance between them than the width of one eye. When too closely set, the face will have an unpleasant expression.

Smoothing the Surface. With the finger tips, gently smooth all rough or bumpy areas. You will need short fingernails, otherwise the face will soon be pockmarked. Keep in mind the fact that the "reasonable facsimile" premise rules out such subtle details as nostrils, eyelids and eyeballs. The smoothing will blend the hills into the valleys. Look at the head from all sides, left, right, top and bottom, and especially from the bottom. In this way you can easily see whether one cheek is fatter than the other, or if the chin is lopsided, or the forehead too bulging.

How to Shape the Lips. The smoothing will produce a rather flat area between the bottom of the nose and the bulge of the chin. It is now the time to add the lips. Take a very small piece of clay and roll it into a tiny sausage that is pointed at both ends. Set it slightly higher than half way between the nose and chin tip. Roll a second tiny sausage, somewhat shorter in length, and set it directly below and touching the first. The thickness of these pieces will determine the fullness or poutiness of the mouth.

The mouth is modeled with the flat end of an orange stick or a small, flat-ended wood modeling tool. Do not use the tool which comes in the box of a child's modeling clay. The proper shape of the tool is shown in the picture on page **139**. With this tool blend the upper roll back and up towards the nose. When satisfied with the appearance of the upper lip, blend the lower roll down much more sharply to form a definite indentation between it and the soft full chin. With the tip of the tool make definite indentations at the corners of the mouth, pointing them upwards slightly. The mouth

MODELED HEADS

Front and side views of clay sketches for doll's heads. A bit more work is needed to finish them before casting. Notice how the boy's head requires thinning on its right side. When viewed straight on the over plumpness is hardly noticeable. When viewed from below, as photographed, such inequalities become very evident. Examine the work from every angle as you progress; top, bottom, each side, front and back.

should be full, even slightly exaggerated, because some of the detail will be lost in the casting. Do not try to model ears. They are not necessary. If the finished doll must have ears it is easy to simulate them afterwards.

Finish Neck and Shoulders. Smooth down the neck taking care not to make it too thin. The reverse curve where the neck joins the shoulder should be quite sharp. The shoulder line is then carried out smoothly to the tip and tapered off. In this kind of work do not try to indicate bones or muscles. Everything should be smooth and soft-looking with the accent on slight plumpness.

Making a Mold. Select a cardboard box somewhat wider, longer and deeper than the measurements of the clay model. It should be of such size as to allow at least three-quarters of an inch of plaster between the tip of the nose of the model and the bottom of the box, the back of the head and the top of the box.

Plaster of Paris is used for the casting material. Pour about a pint of water into a shallow pan or bowl. Then, slowly, pour the plaster into the water until it forms a dry island in the center. Now the mixture may be stirred until the plaster is thoroughly blended with the water. It should be the consistency of thin cream.

Soapy Solution Is Important. Paint the entire head, neck and shoulders of the clay model with very soapy water. Be sure that the soap solution covers every bit of clay. This makes it easy to take the clay model out of the cast after the latter has hardened. Paint the inside of the cardboard box with the soap solution for the same reason. Now fill the box half way with the liquid plaster. Press the bottom of the model against the side of the box and slide it, face down, into the plaster, until plaster reaches half way up the head. Back of head, neck and shoulders are left exposed. Press two soaped marbles half way into the plaster, at opposite corners. Now allow this part of the mold to set and dry.

When first half of mold is dry, take out the marbles but leave clay head in place. Again, soap all exposed parts of plaster as well as the back of head, neck and shoulders. With a fresh solution of plaster and water, fill the box to the top. Allow to set and dry. When dry, tear off the cardboard sides and bottom and lift off the top piece of the cast. If this seems difficult, gently pry the pieces apart with a silver table knife. The seam between the two parts of the mold is easily seen. Slip the knife into the seam and work it around the edges. If the soaping has been thorough the cast will separate perfectly.

Lift out the clay model. Do not try to preserve it. It has served its purpose. Clean out any small bits of clay that may adhere inside the plaster mold. Place the two pieces of the mold together and tie a cord around it. Leave it tied for about a day before actually making a cast.

CASTING A DOLL'S HEAD

A variety of materials may be used to cast a doll's head in a plaster mold. Powdered papier mâché, plastic wood, self-hardening clay, homemade papier mâché, homemade composition, even wax. If you have access to a kiln in which the head may be fired, you can cast the head in ceramic clays.

No matter what the material, the method of casting is the same throughout. Each material offers its own slight difficulties in handling but these are easily overcome after a few moments of experimentation.

The material to be used for casting must be pliable and fairly soft. Before casting, grease the inside of the mold by rubbing it with a soap solution. This is easily done with a wet pastry brush that has been swished around on a cake of soap. Unless a soap solution entirely coats the inside of the mold, the cast will stick and may even require breaking the mold to remove it. The casting material is pressed firmly into each part of the mold with the fingers, making sure every nook and cranny has its quota. Build up this shell in layers, making it not more than a quarter inch thick except for the nose which is best filled solidly. The shell is built up flush with the edge of the mold but not beyond it.

When both pieces of the mold have been filled with the necessary casting material, fit the two pieces together and tie them tightly with strong string bound around all four sides. Set aside to dry. The drying time depends upon the material used. Do not separate mold until you are perfectly sure the cast is completely dry. Cut off string and lift off back of mold. Lift out cast. Do not paint, cover, or decorate it for another twenty-four hours.

CASTING MATERIALS AND HOW TO HANDLE THEM

Powdered papier mâché may be bought in art supply stores or directly from the manufacturer. Follow the directions that come with it. As you gain confidence in modeling, a head may be made of this product by direct modeling rather than by casting. With this method, however, the head so made is necessarily solid which adds considerably to its weight.

Plastic wood is a bit tricky to handle but, with care, makes an extremely satisfactory head. It is very light in weight and practically unbreakable. Plastic wood is sticky to work with, consequently great care must be taken that no air bubbles occur between it and the mold. Keep cleaning the finger tips with plastic wood solvent. A useful tool for pressing it into the mold is the metal ball head of a dial telephone twirler. Place the plastic wood in with the fingers, then tamp it down with the metal ball. Since it comes in various colors, choose white to work with.

Homemade papier mâché works well but is a nuisance to make when you can buy the commercially prepared material. It can be made from torn (not cut) strips of newspaper, about half an inch wide and five or six inches long. The strips are first dipped into warm water and then fitted snugly into the mold. Every strip must overlap the ones beside it and joinings between strips should be staggered brick fashion. When one layer is completed, rub every bit of it with a coating of medium thin wallpaper wheat paste. Lay the first layer of strips horizontally, the second vertically, third, horizontally, etc. Each layer must be rubbed with the paste. At least six layers must be put in to get a reasonably durable head. Do not join the two parts of the mold. Let the papier mâché dry, take them out and trim off the rough edges. Fit them together and join by pasting two strips along the seam. An additional strip, to give strength, may be pasted along the inside of the seam if desired.

THE WEEPING PEASANT WOMAN
This doll is 12 inches tall, and has real hair and a wax face. It was created by Lewis Sorensen of Bremerton, Wash., and shows extraordinary fidelity to details and appearance.

Homemade Compositions. Homemade composition or plastic may be made of several things. A salt, cornstarch and hot water solution dries quite hard and is fairly durable, especially when covered with paint or a fabric "skin." To make it:

Mix one part salt with three parts cornstarch. Blend thoroughly.

Add one part boiling water and mix. Knead into a dough.

Press it into the mold. Allow at least a week to dry.

Wood flour (an extremely fine sawdust) and clear lacquer is another homemade composition. Enough lacquer is added and stirred into the wood flour to moisten it and hold it together. The result should be like pie crust dough. Work quickly as the lacquer dries very rapidly. Press it into the mold, keeping the finger tips clean with lacquer thinner. Do not use this near a stove or other fire. The mold is not joined together. Let the two parts dry thoroughly, remove and then join together, using a bit of this plastic along the edges to make the seam. Tie back and front of cast together with a strip of gauze bandage. Let dry over night.

If you like to experiment, try making up your own composition. Many of the old patents for dolls' heads included the ingredients (not the quantities for mixing) that were used to make their composition. For instance, the composition for the Mason & Taylor heads was made of glue, rosin, plaster of Paris and another ingredient (probably bran), mixed to a dough, rolled out like a cookie and then pressed inside the mold. Other compositions used flour in place of bran and eliminated the powdered rosin. Try crack filler, a water putty, and mix with cold water to a dough consistency.

Using Semi-Liquid Casting Materials. The technique for making a head of wax, plaster of Paris or ceramic clay is somewhat different than the preceding methods. First fit the two pieces of the mold together and hold them by tightly tied string or carefully applied strips of adhesive tape. The three materials mentioned above are very liquid and must be poured into the mold through the bottom. Since doll head molds are small, entirely fill the mold, which has been thoroughly soaped inside, allow it to set for a moment or two; then pour out the excess material. This will produce a thin shell. To thicken it, pour in a second supply, then pour it out after a min-

THREE MORMON PIONEER FIGURES

This group was modeled by Mr. Sorensen and is on permanent display in the Utah State
Capitol. The figures, while not photographic, are based upon actual people who settled
Salt Lake City, and are costumed in fabrics furnished by their descendants. The man is
18 inches tall. The dolls show the great skill of their designer as well as mastery of material.

ute or two. When wax and plaster of Paris are hard (leave overnight), they are done and ready for decoration. Liquid ceramic clay, when hard, must be removed from the mold and set aside for thorough drying before firing.

Plaster of Paris may be bought in any hardware store. Modeling wax may be bought in art supply stores or by mail from the advertisers in *Hobbies* magazine. Ceramic clays may be bought from art supply stores and advertisers in *Hobbies* and *School Arts* magazines.

DECORATING THE FINISHED CAST

Any roughnesses or bits of excess material must be removed from the cast head. The finest grade sandpaper may be lightly used on all casting materials except wax. When the surface is quite smooth, rub it with a cloth saturated in alcohol to remove any soap that may still be on it. The soap, being greasy, will spoil the paint or other "skin" applied to the face.

How to Use an Enamel Coat. A high grade enamel is used for the base coat. To achieve a good skin tone mix a small bit of clear red, a tiny dab of burnt sienna with a teaspoon full of turpentine. When completely blended, mix this drop by drop into about half a cup of ivory enamel. Stir thoroughly between drops so that the tone may be watched. Avoid making too rosy or too dark a color. Flow the enamel on the doll head and set aside to dry. The features are painted on with artist's oil paints.

Skin Made of Fabric or Kidskin. "Skin" may be applied to the head in the form of fabric, kidskin or wax. When a fabric is used, it should be quite thin, definitely stretchable and of a color that is a fair approximation of real skin. Applying skin is a tricky procedure requiring patience. The head is first coated with vegetable glue, then the material is centered on the face and stroked and fitted so that all parts of it adhere to the head without wrinkles or bulges. If the fabric is woven, place it so that the weave runs on the bias. This is not necessary when using a thin cotton or thin wool-knit jersey.

Very thin kidskin, such as used in evening gloves, makes a beautiful skin. Be sure, however, that it is *not* glacé kidskin. Use the very supple, dull kidskin and be sure the hands are perfectly clean while working with it. It, too, must be persuaded by gentle stretching and working, to fit into every crevice and depression. The kidskin is left natural color and the features painted directly on it in delicate tones with oil paint.

Coating the Head with Wax. Another method of finishing the modeled head is by coating it with wax. A base coat of skin-colored enamel is put on the modeled head. When dry, the features are painted on, using very bright colors. They will show through the wax coating which softens the colors. Use either commercially prepared modeling wax or pure beeswax, not melted down candles or paraffine. The best way is to dip the entire head into the wax rather than pouring it on. The dipping insures an even coating but requires a rather generous supply of the material so that the entire head may be coated in one dip. Two or three coats of wax should be used. Dip and set aside to harden. Re-dip and set aside. If the beeswax looks too brown in color it may be lightened in tone by adding some melted, pure wax, candle. This type of candle may be bought in a religious supply store. The candles for table use do not work out satisfactorily.

Applied skin should cover only the face up to slightly above the hairline, the neck and shoulders. If it proves too difficult to work the fabric onto the shoulders, avoid complications by ending the material just slightly below the neck. The doll's clothes will cover the parts that have not been complexioned.

When the doll head is finished it may be glued to the body just as were the antique heads. Use plastic glue for this purpose, spreading it on the shoulders of the body and on the inner side of the shoulder piece of the doll head. Press head firmly onto body and tie in place with gauze bandages.

Dress the doll as desired, knowing that your skill has produced a unique and beautiful doll that may some day be a collector's item. You have your mold to duplicate it and the second and successive dolls will go much more quickly because you are becoming more familiar with the materials and more adept in handling them.

PORTRAIT DOLLS

Sooner or later the urge to try one's hand at creating a portrait doll overtakes practically every doll maker. Perhaps you wish to create a likeness of your own baby son or young daughter. It can be done, of course, by a trained sculptor or portrait artist. However, even the majority of trained artists find it most difficult to capture an exact resemblance. The talented amateur can, with work and experimentation, achieve the effect of a fairly good resemblance between a doll and a child because the doll-form of artistic expression is viewed with indulgence. The public looks at the finished work expecting to be pleased and surprised and usually is if a few basic rules are followed by the doll artist.

Analyzing Dominant Features. Look at a small child, preferably one you've never seen before, and what is the first thing you notice? The color and style of its hair and then its eyes. Because the child looks back at you, the eyes hold your attention more than the other features. Could you, after five minutes, tell whether the mouth was large, the nose long or short? But you could quite accurately tell whether the cheeks were pink, pale or ruddy, the eyes dark or light, the hair blonde, brown or reddish. So it would seem that a child's coloring is the most distinctive feature and one to be followed accurately by the doll portraitist.

Study the Eyes. After the coloring, really scrutinize the child's eyes. What shape are they? Compare them with the shape of your own eyes and those of other members of the family. The upper eyelid is the one to examine, for it determines the shape of the eye—oval, rounded or almond-shaped. The amount and placing of the eyelashes tend to emphasize this special characteristic of the eye. In your scrutiny, try to see the lid as it seems to be under the influencing shadow of the lashes. The color of the eyes and the size of the iris (how much or how little of the white is visible?) is a problem to be met when painting the finished head. The distance between the eyes is something to be decided upon now and followed when modeling.

PORTRAIT DOLL OF THOMAS JEFFERSON

The face shows an exceptional resemblance to the distinguished Virginian, and the clothing of both dolls is authentic for the period.

PORTRAIT DOLL OF WALTER HAMPDEN

This doll is costumed exactly as the famous actor appeared in his role of Cyrano de Ber
gerac. It has real hair and a built-up nose. The Walter Hampden and Ed Wynn dolls wer
created by Mary Green for the theatrical collection of Daniel Blum.

PORTRAIT DOLL OF ED WYNN

The well known comedian is represented accurately in this doll in one of his familiar roles
as funny man.

A Child's Nose. The childish nose has a bland way of melting into the cheeks, with few children having anything distinguished or characteristic about the nose shape. Your subject, however, may be different, so really look at the nose. Concentrate on the tip. Is it pug, straight, fat, or just a nose? Are the nostrils large, small, indifferent, flared? Is the base of the nose (where it joins the upper lip) wide or narrow?

The Mouth Takes Skill. The mouth is an extremely important feature that has defied true representation by many a professional. It is most difficult for the amateur to model a widely smiling or open mouth. Do not try it, even if it is the most characteristic expression of the child. Compare the width of the closed mouth with the width of the base of the nose. Is it wider or the same? Are the corners deeply indented, the lips full, thin, well-defined?

How about the chin? Is it pointed, rounded, fat or dimpled?

Determine General Shape of Face and Head. The shape of the face and head, when accurately portrayed, can be a very strong factor in achieving a striking resemblance. One's skill in depicting individual features may be a bit weak but the all-over impression of resemblance can be emphasized by a strong portrayal of the general contours. Is the face square, oval, pointed? Is the head rounded on top or rather flat? A slight exaggeration of these shapes is all to the good when you come to modeling them.

MAKING THE PORTRAIT HEAD

Build an egg-shaped clay oval in the same way you did when making "just a doll's head." Set it firmly on a short but strong neck. Remember, the blunt end of the egg is the crown of the head, the pointed end the chin. At the exact middle of the oval draw a line right across the front of the head. That is to remind you to keep the features *below* that line. Build up the features as explained in the beginning of this chapter. Do not dig out cavities but form them by building up the surrounding areas with small flat bits of clay. Roughly model the eyes, nose, cheeks, mouth and chin. Work on both sides of the face simultaneously.

A Little Exaggeration. The resemblance will begin to appear sooner than you expect if you have the answers in your mind to the questions posed in the preceding paragraphs. Exaggerate the dominant features just a bit more than is truly lifelike because some of that exaggeration will be lost during the mold taking and final casting.

When to Stop Modeling. When the resemblance is "pretty good," both to you and someone else, stop modeling! That resemblance is going to be intensified by the painting of the face and features and by the hair. Too many "pretty good" resemblances have been hopelessly lost because the modeler did not know when to cease. Those few extra strokes, designed to perfect, too often destroy. Leave well enough alone and move on to the next step, that of making the cast.

Over and above the resemblance captured in both the modeling and the coloring of the portrait head, is the enhanced effect gained by dressing the doll in a miniature duplicate of the child's favorite dress. That truly completes the portrait.

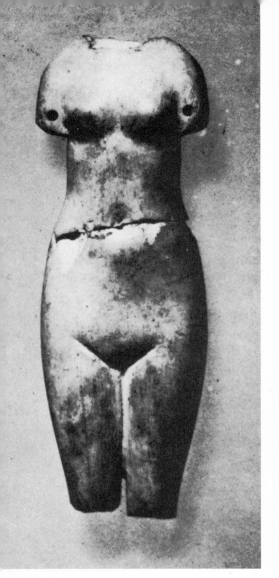

Left: IVORY DOLL

This figure was modeled in ancient Babylonia, and resembles modern sculpture.

Right: DOLL OF CARVED BONE

A product of Tarentum, Italy, made in the third century, B.C.

7.

The Story of Dolls

THERE ARE, IN CERTAIN MUSEUMS THROUGHOUT THE WORLD, examples of dolls that date back to over four thousand years B.C. While it is obvious that some of these examples really are dolls, many of these so-called dolls are actually fetishes, or religious objects and representations of various gods.

There is no question about the Greek dolls being dolls, i.e., playthings made expressly for the use of little girls. Not only were dolls made specifically as toys but they were made in large enough quantities to warrant being sold in special shops devoted to that type of merchandise alone. That this is no picturesque fancy on the part of doll-romanticists is testified to by the fact that scientific excavations have uncovered remains of those shops, have discovered fragments that leave no other conclusion to be drawn.

Ancient Sculptors Carved Dolls. The two dolls shown here are several thousand years old. The Babylonian ivory doll bears an extraordinary resemblance to modern sculpture. It is obviously the product of a master craftsman. The other doll on the same page is equally interesting in its extreme antiquity if not in beauty. This Roman lady (from Tarentum, third century B.C.) is of carved bone and has arms and legs not too dissimilar from those of her descendants of the nineteenth century. Notice, too, the similarity in her hair-do with that of many dolls made between 1820 and 1830.

Long Ago Dolls Became Big Business. From that dim past to the present day, dolls have enjoyed a double role: the cherished plaything of millions of little girls and, more recently, the equally cherished and collected plaything of thousands of adults. Dolls, commercially speaking, have been big business for some five hundred years. It is a business that continues to grow not only in the number of dolls being manufactured but in the amount of money being spent.

Homemade Dolls Ranked Among the Finest. Some of the finest dolls in the world, however, are the product of the home doll maker. While many professional artists and sculptors have turned their skill and talents into the design and making of dolls, the quality of workmanship and beauty that is intrinsic in many homemade dolls is equal to that of the finest professional work.

Whether you collect (buy other people's work) or make your own dolls, the enjoyment derived will be considerably heightened by increasing your knowledge of the dolls of all ages. Professionally made or created by the amateur, practically any doll has an interesting, if mute, background and story. The story unfolds as you recognize the subtle as well as the obvious clues that each doll carries.

Among the oldest dolls appearing in many doll collections are ones that originally were made for religious purposes. Individually, or in groups, they were designed to represent primitive gods or symbols. The most outstanding of these are those figures created to represent the leading figures of the Christmas story.

NATIVITY GROUPS OR CRÈCHE FIGURES

Representing the Virgin and Child, with Joseph, the Shepherds and the Wise Men, the Crèche or Nativity Group was always a very special artistic creation by professional artists and craftsmen. The modeling or carving of each figure was both a work of love as well as of art. Every effort was bent towards making the figures as realistic as possible. The faces had real beauty and sweetness while retaining a characteristic ruggedness and strength. The most outstanding feature of all the figures was the wonderfully expressive hands. With the exception of the Virgin whose folded hands were usually hidden by a voluminous cape or cloak or were folded on her breast, all hands were modeled with fingers distended and palms turned towards the Child. The hands express wonder, amazement, awe. The Nativity Groups belonging to wealthy churches were magnificently costumed. Those of poorer churches were dressed less richly and splendidly.

A Lovely Group from Italy. Two quite different interpretations of the Crèche are presented here. The first one is part of a large group made in the eighteenth century in a small town near Naples, Italy. The Virgin stands gazing down. Her cloak is that lovely shade of soft blue that is always associated with Mary. Underneath the cape are clothes of the period. The shepherds are dressed in typical rough garments and jackets. Included in this group (but not shown) are the other main participants as well as a large group of townspeople who came to pay homage. Made of clay, the faces, lower arms and legs have a definite sheen, probably due to polishing with a slip stone, an ancient method of endowing clay with a subtle satiny luster. The bodies are of wire and straw bound together to give bulk. The main characters range from twelve to sixteen inches in height. The townspeople are eight and ten inches high.

A Cape Cod Artist. The second Nativity group shown is the work of the artist Florence Bradshaw Brown of Cape Cod, Massachusetts. Well known for her gay and charming water-color illustrations of children, Mrs. Brown has recently turned to the creation of "figures." With great skill and a wonderful sense of design and color, her character and story-book figures are delightfully modeled

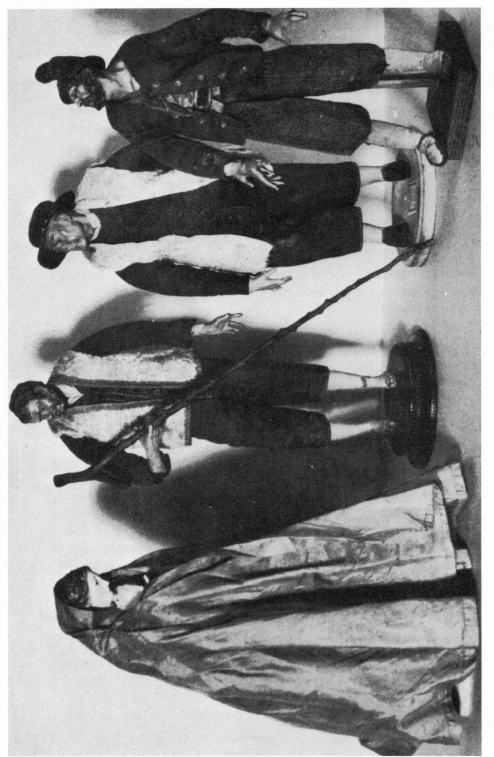

FIGURES OF THE CRÈCHE This group was created in Naples in the eighteenth century. The bodies were constructed of wire and straw

MODERN NATIVITY GROUP. These figures were designed by Florence Bradshaw Brown of Cape Cod, Mass. Dressed in rough fabrics, the group has a humble simplicity, and a warm, tender quality.

and beautifully costumed. Her Crèche has the simple and humble quality that is consonant with the characters. Dressed in the rough, drab fabrics more truly representative of the original costumes, Mary and Joseph display warmth and tender wonder. The placing of the animals, also modeled by Mrs. Brown, serves to frame the composition and to focus attention on the Child.

A Distinguishing Feature. Nativity Groups have been made for over five hundred years. Like many other forms of religious art many of them have disappeared during the stress of war. Individual Crèche figures have reappeared dressed as dolls and, as such, have found their way into museums and private collections. The initiated have always recognized them for what they were but many a Crèche figure is still classified as a "doll." The identifying feature which distinguishes these figures from ordinary dolls is the modeling and position of the hands. Look for the outward turned palms, the definitely distended fingers, the completely adult appearance of the hands.

DOLLS FROM THE FIFTEENTH CENTURY

As far back as the fifteenth century dolls were being made commercially in Germany. Old engravings show artisans working on dolls which were of clay and rather crudely modeled. Carved wooden dolls also appeared about the same time. As time progressed, methods of manufacture improved and volume increased. A primitive form of the assembly line was introduced when the demand for dolls became pressing. While still entirely handmade, the doll became the product of many hands rather than the entire work of one person. Specialization had set in. One man would make nothing but legs and arms, another would concentrate on heads and bodies. Still a third person would paint the dolls. As doll designing increased in realistic detail, a greater number of people took part in making them.

Dolls Were Court Favorites. By the seventeenth and eighteenth centuries doll making and doll costuming had reached such heights that the leading artists of various countries were often

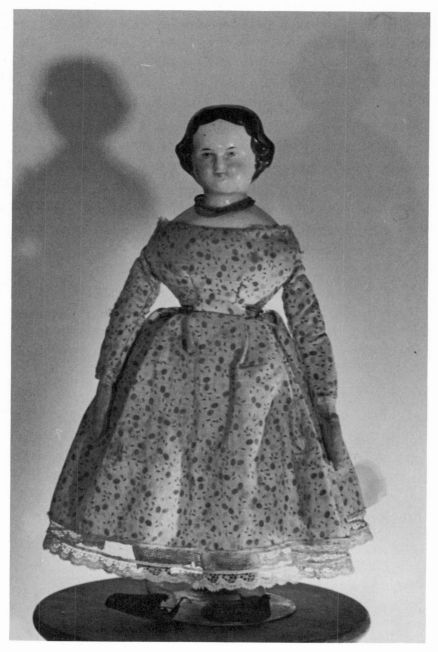

A most delicate pink tone is embodied in the china head and deep sloping shoulders of this delightful little doll. Her homemade body and original clothing are charming if rather inexpertly made and extremely fragile. The necklace is made of tiny turquoise-colored beads. She was found wrapped in newspaper in an old trunk bought by the author a good many years ago at an auction on Cape Cod. She dates from somewhere in the late 1830's or early 40's.

commissioned to make designs specifically for dolls. Kings and courtiers had lavishly costumed and bejeweled dolls made as gifts. The greatest skill and the richest fabrics went into these creations. They were used both as political tokens of good will, and as fashion indicators designed to prepare visiting or betrothed royalty for the styles of a particular court. These dolls are interesting as a record of their times, and their value is shown by the fabulous charges for their purchase.

Paris the Fashion Center for Dolls. Naturally, dolls in that class were few in number. On the other hand, the mere fact of their existence stimulated many artists and craftsmen, particularly in Paris, towards making and costuming the more common doll as beautifully as possible. By the eighteenth century there was an appreciable number of shops in Paris devoted exclusively to the costuming of dolls and an even greater number of craftsmen specializing in the making of specific fashion accessories such as gloves, bonnets and hats, shoes, etc. The culmination in this manufacturing of doll wardrobes came during the 1870's when the well-dressed doll from Paris was equipped with upwards of a hundred garments and fashion accessories.

Along with this professional manufacture of dolls and their costumes went the home manufacture that satisfied countless numbers of little girls. Many of these home products were distinguished by beautiful workmanship and needlework, just as many of them, to the modern eye, seem anything but pretty. But all were cherished and loved to death, thus accounting for the very few specimens of them that have been preserved.

The Backbone of Today's Collections. The dolls of the nineteenth century are the ones that are, perhaps, of greatest interest to the average person. Many are still available and others are turning up with a fair degree of frequency. As interest in doll collecting increases, more and more attics and trunks are being examined for possible finds. These are the dolls that make up the backbone of most doll collections. Their background and history is given in the following pages.

WILLIAMANNA

She is a composition shoulder-head doll of a type that is sometimes called "pumpkin head" because of the style of the hair-do. Body is homemade but arms are modern commercial replacements of white kid. Her own arms had been badly chewed up by mice. Her embroidered cotton underwear, probably original, are of much better workmanship than her red wool gown that is trimmed with black velvet ribbon. The dress was made a good twenty years after the doll was first bought. She dates from the 1870's. Dating old dolls from their clothes is tricky despite the honest belief that they may be original. Sewing machines were in fairly common use during the 1860's (Williamanna's clothes are machine stitched); however, the handsewn garments of later dolls, particularly those originating in rural areas, is often used as a guide to dating, which is a mistake. Also remember that doll clothes often survived the doll and were used for new and later dolls.

A GREINER COMPOSITION SHOULDER-HEAD DOLL

She is in excellent condition. The only indisputable proof of
whether a doll is a Greiner is its label. Greiner's patent was for the
composition (taken out in 1858). He used German molds for his
heads. When the patent expired his formula was adopted by a
number of other manufacturers.

8.

What Goes Into Doll Collections

DOLL COLLECTING IS FUN! IT CAN BE AS EXPENSIVE OR as modest as you want. There are no rules or regulations to inhibit your fancies other than those imposed by your pocketbook and your good sense. It is a hobby that one seldom, if ever, tires of because of the infinite variety of examples to be studied, coveted, perhaps bought or even duplicated by your own agile fingers. The more you learn about types, probable ages, costuming and hairdos, the keener becomes your interest in discovering and recognizing new examples. That you also gain a wide perception and appreciation of the manners and customs of other peoples of the world, both contemporary and of days gone by, is a plus value that is picked up as you go along.

AMAZING GROWTH OF A HOBBY

The American world has become astonishingly doll conscious within a relatively short time. It is estimated that there are well over two hundred and twenty-five million dolls in this country, both antique and modern, foreign and domestic. The number grows each year. As a hobby, doll collecting has gained impetus and importance as rapidly as any other form of collecting. Naturally enough, such a rapid growth in interest and purchasing power has brought an equally alive and interested group of people who are ready to supply the doll collector with attractive items. Before you know it the charms of a certain doll, accompanied by the persuasive sales talk of the dealer, will have proved sufficiently attractive to make you buy it. Your "buy" may be a good one; but then again you may sometimes be considerably more extravagant than was wise.

HOW DO GREAT COLLECTIONS START?

Many of the great doll collections, both private and in museums or other public institutions, started accidentally. The nucleus of a collection often is a doll or two that originated in one's own childhood or came as a gift from an older person who had treasured it for various reasons. Of no great value, other than that implicit in its personal associations, such dolls offer a very good focal point about which to build a small group or collection.

For Children's Charities. A famous collection started some fifty years ago because some children asked a talented but amateur doll maker to lend them her dolls for an exhibition. The children intended to sell tickets for the exhibition and use the proceeds for a local charity. The doll maker loaned the dolls but went considerably further. She collected over two thousand dolls within a few years for the sole purpose of exhibition to raise money for children's charities. This collection traveled all over the country. Another well known collection came into being as a release from grief at the loss of a young daughter. Many less important, but equally interesting, collections have grown through a child's interest having been made known to interested adults. Older people who travel extensively need little excuse to purchase dolls in far corners of the world as gifts for young friends or relatives. The reason for a collection may be nothing more than "because I like dolls" and that is reason enough.

Above: These unbelievably tiny dolls (⅞ of an inch high) are made of silk wrapped wire. Elaborate and authentically detailed costumes need a magnifying glass to be appreciated. They were made in Mexico in the early 20th century. *Below:* These wittily exaggerated 5 inch tall dolls from Portugal are made of felt with hard faces. Carefully detailed regional costumes are accurate. Made in the late 1950's, they are excellent candidates for a collection of foreign dolls.

The flirtatious señorita, carrying a miniature prayer book and rosary, is one of a large group of satirically designed Spanish dolls that began to appear in the 1950's. They come in both contemporary and folk costumes, beautifully designed and with five accessories.

A 1962 stump (no legs) doll from Sardinia is handsomely gowned in silk, velvet, lace and embroidered blouse and ribbon trim. Hands and face are of brown felt.

WHERE TO FIND OUT ABOUT DOLLS

Even if money is no object do not be too ready to buy dolls. A good part of the fun lies in shopping around, learning the comparative values, seeing what other shops or dealers have to offer. There are innumerable places where you may study and examine actual dolls, as in museums, for instance.

Museums Are Not Dry As Dust. Many more art museums have doll collections than you would imagine. It is true that not all museums having these collections keep them on permanent display, although some of them do. Ask at the information desk for both the actual collection and for any written or pictorial matter the museum may have prepared for sale to the public. Sometimes these collections are quite small. Other collections are of great variety and scope. It may be surprising to find them under the same roof with Rembrandt paintings, Rodin sculptures or rare porcelains. They are there because in their own individual fashion they, too, are illustrative of the cultures of past ages as well as of contemporary arts.

The number of historical or antique societies that maintain historical houses, small museums or other buildings is very large. Frequently, these houses include a few dolls among the furniture and personal items on exhibit. Battered or beautiful, such dolls are extremely interesting to see and many of them have entertaining stories attached to them. Get the custodian or attendant to talk about them if there is no explanatory card attached to the doll. Who was the original owner of the doll? What is it made of? Are the clothes original? What kind of underclothes is it wearing? Does it have a name? A few simple questions will usually unlock a flood of information.

Ask Your Librarian or Teacher. Sometimes the Children's Rooms of Public Libraries own various kinds of dolls that are used for seasonal display. Talk to the librarian in charge. It is not at all unusual to find that a backstage view of the dolls may be arranged for. She also can advise you on books that you may find interesting and informative. That they come off the shelves in the Children's

Room does not necessarily mean that they are juvenile. A tremendous amount of educational work is being done in schools all over the country through the study of dolls, consequently libraries are acquiring a surprising amount of source material for reference work. You, too, can make profitable use of such books and articles.

Antique shops and shows and doll hospitals have a lot to offer. While they are primarily concerned with doing business, your interest and desire to learn about dolls usually will produce an equally interested response. Many antique dealers have succumbed to the fascination of dolls. It is often the case that they have reserved their choicest finds for themselves. Like all collectors, however, they love to talk about their own hobby. That kind of talk inevitably calls for concrete illustrations and before you know it, some of those choice dolls may be brought out to emphasize various points under discussion.

It is equally true, however, that many antique shop proprietors sell old dolls simply because there is a demand for them. Dolls, to them, are just another commodity that the public wants. This type of dealer has neither the time nor the inclination to study dolls. His information is usually superficial and often inaccurate. Without too much background of your own in the field of dolls, it is quite simple to recognize that fact and to determine that there would be little to learn from that particular source.

WHERE DO OLD DOLLS COME FROM?

Naturally, your friends will soon find out about your new enthusiasm for dolls. Some of those friends may even be able to put you on the track of "really old" dolls. Attics, old trunks, forgotten bureaus and chests have a way of harboring quaint and sometimes lovely examples. Such finds, while not too frequent, add to the zest of the game.

Remember, however, that the majority of the really valuable dolls have already been picked up by collectors or have been donated to museums or historical societies. Much more frequent than any valuable discoveries are the apocryphal stories that accompany almost any doll that looks old. Take all such stories with a grain of salt. They are not told with the intent to deceive but

"BABY" DOLL

This doll was dressed in Holland, with infant's bonnet and long silk dress elaborately
trimmed with tucking and lace.

are a natural build-up of interest or an honestly mistaken set of facts based on faulty memories or inaccurate statements from some one else.

An Example of a Hoax. I experienced a perfect example of this not long ago. I asked a friend if she had any interesting dolls. In no sense of the word could she be called a doll collector, yet I dropped the question simply to see what would come of it. Yes, she had a doll "well over a hundred years old!" It was a very interesting doll, because it had come from Holland, and had been given to her when she was a little girl by a woman who said it had been her grandmother's.

This all sounded most interesting, so I requested an immediate interview between the doll and myself. It is a charming little thing as can be seen by looking at its pictures shown here. Having a swivel bisque head with blown glass eyes, and a papier mâché body, it could not have been dated much earlier than the 1880's. Dressed as a Dutch baby, its clothes were delicate and beautifully made. However, when the doll was undressed, it had a label on its stomach that read:

Charles Morrell
50 Burlington Arcade, London

What the Clues Revealed. Obviously, the doll originated in London and probably was sent to Holland where it was dressed or redressed. Another amusing note lies in the fact that the doll was designed to represent a much older child than an infant. This is illustrated by the fact that under its crocheted bootees are legs and feet upon which are modeled short socks and double strapped slippers with definite heels. This fact immediately revises the first estimate of 1880's, bringing the dating of the doll into the 20th century. Why? Little girls, before the 20th century, did not wear socks or slippers styled like these.

Inaccuracies of this sort, when you recognize them as such, lend piquancy and excitement to the study and collection of dolls.

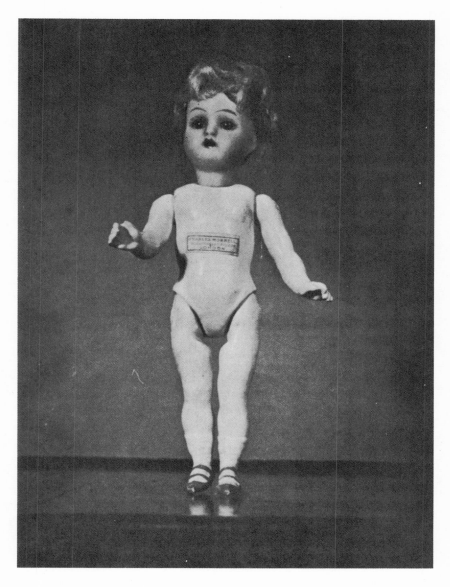

A CLOSER INSPECTION

When "baby" was undressed, the footwear and maker's name change first impressions. Doll **has** bisque head, papier mâché body, and is owned by Mrs. Herman Lazarus, Clinton, N. J.

DOLLS ARE EASILY CLASSIFIED ACCORDING TO MATERIAL

It requires no expert knowledge or prolonged study to determine the materials from which dolls are made. Ancient dolls, dating in some instances as far back as three and four thousand years B.C., are made of clay, bone, ivory, wood, linen rags, bound papyrus, stone, etc. The dolls the average person is concerned with are of considerably later vintage. In fact, ninety-nine out of a hundred dolls are considerably less than one hundred years old. Despite their age (a subject which is discussed at length later on) or youth, it is simple to classify dolls into broad groups determined as:

> wood
> wax
> papier mâché or composition
> china, bisque, Parian
> leather
> rubber
> celluloid
> rag
> novelties

The above classification of dolls is extremely simple and a rather obvious one. Naturally, even the most inexpert person will realize that such broad classifications must be broken down in order to bring the picture into focus.

MAJORITY OF OLD DOLLS ARE OF FOREIGN ORIGIN

Despite the fact that there were so-called doll manufacturers in this country early in the nineteenth century, no real manufacturing of dolls existed here until about the middle of that century. All professionally made dolls, no matter of what material, were imported from Germany, France and England, with the German importations far exceeding those of the other European countries. Entire dolls, doll heads, doll eyes and arms and legs and bodies, were brought into this country in enormous quantities. When one or more persons were engaged in the business of assembling doll parts they were termed doll manufacturers. They were sold here either as a complete doll or as doll heads for which bodies were made at home.

The German Toymakers. As early as the fourteenth century Germany was the leader in the doll business. Clay dolls were produced in substantial quantities by local German craftsmen, assembled at Nuremberg and from there shipped to all parts of Europe. About the fifteenth century, wooden dolls began to appear. Made in the mountain districts of Germany and Austria, they were rather crude, although they had jointed arms and legs. These wooden dolls soon superseded the clay dolls in popularity and, by the time of Queen Elizabeth's reign (1558–1603), were quite common in England.

Early Wood Dolls. It is a matter of record that one of these wood dolls was brought to this country in 1583 and was presented to a small Indian girl by a member of Sir Walter Raleigh's expedition. The presentation was documented by John White, artist of the expedition. Apparently this doll was not alone in its travels, for the book written in 1583 concerning the expedition says that the little Indian girls "were delighted with the puppets and babes brought out of England." The plural form indicates that quite a few must have accompanied this first expedition.

Dolls Portrayed by Famous Artists. It is this same type of wood doll, very little changed other than in the clothes it wears, that appears in so many child and family portraits of the seventeenth and eighteenth centuries painted by English, French, Dutch and American artists. John Singleton Copley, one of Boston's most famous artists, painted his own family shortly after the Boston Tea Party. In the lower left hand corner of the canvas lies one of these wooden dolls dressed exactly like his young daughter Elizabeth. This painting now hangs in the National Gallery of Art in Washington, D. C., and is but one of the many famous paintings in which early wood dolls are depicted.

Many Wooden Dolls. Early wood dolls came, for the most part, from around Sonneberg, Germany. They varied in size from three-quarters of an inch to about sixteen inches. The larger they were, the more detailed was the carving of the features and hands. Unlike other types of dolls, these jointed wood dolls made little or no concession to the fluctuating styles. Infrequently, one comes across a variation in the hair styling. These variations are for the most part confined to a single period, 1810–1835. Before and after that period the hair-do is practically identical, consisting entirely of black paint on a slightly pointed or an almost completely round skull with a slight indication of a center part shown at the forehead.

England, too, was producing wood dolls but not in any quantity comparable with the German ones. The best example of the English wood dolls are those called after Queen Anne (1665–1714), not because they looked like her but because they were popular during her period. The better dolls were often finished with a thin plaster coating and had inset glass eyes. Human hair was used to make their wigs. They were elaborately and beautifully dressed, duplicating the fashions of the times. Examples of these dolls are quite rare and, for the most part, are owned by large museums.

From the last quarter of the eighteenth century on through the nineteenth century, the German wood dolls in all sizes became known as "Penny Woodens" because they were sold for a penny in the old "Cent Shops" in New England. Nathaniel Hawthorne, in *The House of the Seven Gables* speaks of these little dolls as "Dutch wooden milkmaids." Whether he actually meant that they originated in Holland, or used the word "Dutch" colloquially to designate German, is a moot point. The fact remains, however, that the same style of doll was being produced in Austria and the Netherlands simultaneously with those of German production.

Young Victoria's Dolls. The Netherlands wood doll was sent to England where one hundred and thirty-two of them found their way into the doll collection of Queen Victoria prior to her ascending the English throne (1837). As a child, Queen Victoria dressed many of these dolls and played with them until she was

LETITIA PENN, an early 18th century wood doll with glass eyes
and carved bamboo hands (at least one of them) supposedly was
owned by William Penn's daughter. Her once handsome gown
shows fine period styling as well as the ravages of time.

fourteen years old. She preferred them to the more realistic dolls that were then beginning to appear.

Quite naturally, many wood dolls were made by Americans at home. Some of them undoubtedly were close facsimiles of the imported dolls, while others were but very crude attempts. Of the so-called Penny Woodens now extant, there is no absolute way of telling which are imported and which are American copies. That they were copied here, and exceedingly well done, goes almost without saying, for their styling is of the simplest, and no great skill or talent was required to duplicate the primitive painting of the features. The New Englander's skill with the jack-knife would have had no trouble in duplicating a Penny Wooden.

Harvest of Dolls in Winter Time. Up until about the middle of the nineteenth century all wood dolls were hand carved. In the earliest days of their career, an entire doll was made by one person. They were a home industry in Germany, made by mountain families in the winter time. As soon as Spring broke, packs of these dolls were sent to the large clearing centers of Sonneberg or Nuremberg from whence they were exported all over the world. As the demand for them increased, the work became more specialized. One member of the family would carve the head and torso, another would do just legs, while a third turned out nothing but arms. The painting of the heads and features became the specialty of still another person. In this way an entire family, from the young children to the grandparents, devoted the winter time to an extremely specialized form of work. A charming picture of this work is given in Margaret Morley's book, *Donkey John of the Toy Valley.* The technical details in the story are based on the author's experiences, living in one of the mountain valleys whose people were winter-time toy makers.

The American Made Wood Doll. This kind of doll, following the hundreds of home whittled Penny Woodens, reached its apogee with the mid-19th century patented doll by Joel Ellis of Springfield, Vt. Green maple wood was steamed until soft, then pressed in molds under tremendous pressure. Not a great many of them were made, perhaps because of the competition offered by the lovely and highly realistic bisque dolls coming into the country from French and German manufacturers.

Wood as a medium for the creation of dolls has retained a devoted coterie of doll artists who prefer to work in that medium. Marion L. Perkins' "Peggity Dolls," modern adaptations of Penny Woodens, Avis Lee's "Tykes," the wood dolls of Darcy (Ruth Williams) and Helen Bullard are all interesting 20th century examples of wood carving and are quite desirable from the collector's point of view. All hand carved wood dolls are originals, therefore their relative scarcity contributes to their desirability.

WAX DOLLS

Wax was one of the earliest modeling materials ever used. Even before the Golden Age in Greece, small wax figures were made as dolls for Greek children. It is a material that has been modeled by the world's greatest sculptors and artists. Easily worked, a good wax can closely approximate the texture and color of human skin. Between the end of the Roman Empire and the fourteenth century, dolls seem to have experienced their own Dark Ages. Then they come on the scene again and it is known that by the sixteenth century, wax was again being experimented with in the manufacture of dolls. By the seventeenth century the method of working wax was so perfected that quantities of French fashion dolls were being made in Paris of this very fragile material.

The First Penny Dolls. There are three types of wax dolls: solid wax, poured wax, and wax over a composition or metal foundation. In all three types, except for the "baby" dolls, only the heads are of wax. It is extremely rare to find wax legs and feet; not so rare are wax hands. Bodies are of cloth or kid to which the wax parts are attached. The "baby" dolls were frequently entirely of wax, often crudely modeled and, on the whole, quite unattractive. Some of these wax baby dolls also are called penny dolls because that was their price in the nineteenth century.

The larger wax "lady" doll was frequently very beautiful. Great care and workmanship was exerted in making her. Her hair, in the more expensive models, was human and inserted hair by hair into her wax scalp. Less expensive models had the hair in-

WAX DOLL FROM PARIS

Bought in Paris in 1849, this doll wears her original clothes. Human hair was inserted
into slit on top of head. Arms have dark kid gloves; body is cloth and face is wax over
composition.

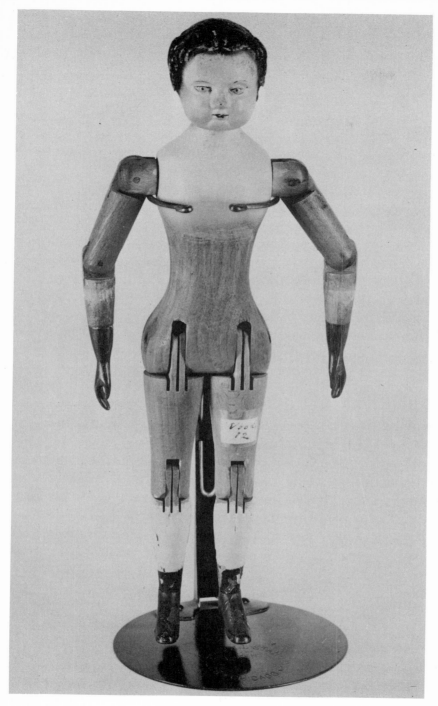

JOEL ELLIS DOLL

Patented in 1873, the Joel Ellis wood doll is a highly sophisticated version of the Penny Woodens. His distinctive joints gave the doll great mobility. The metal boots were always black but sometimes the metal hands were painted white.

serted through a center slit in the head from which it fell in more or less natural strands. This method of coiffing was possible only in the poured wax styles wherein the head was hollow. The wax-over-composition doll sometimes had its hair modeled in the material, other times it was finished with a wig. All types of wax dolls are seen with wigs, as well.

England Excelled in Beautiful Wax Dolls. The most beautiful wax dolls were of English make. Germany, too, made them but excelled the English only in the glass eyes. The English glass eyes never achieved the beauty or realistic quality of those of German manufacture, so it is not surprising to find that many of the English dolls were equipped with German eyes. The exportation from Germany of various doll parts, to be assembled and sold by another country, was a quite common practice. The skill of the German workman, coupled with the much lower wages he demanded, made it commercially unprofitable for other countries to try to compete in various specialized lines.

Considering the fragility of the wax doll, an amazing number of them have survived the ravages of time and the carelessness of various owners. The French Fashion dolls, naturally, were seldom used as playthings, so the excellence of their condition is not to be wondered at. The more ordinary wax doll, designed for children's enjoyment, has really had a hard time of it. That there are so many of them would seem to indicate that they were manufactured and exported to this country in rather large numbers. Perhaps they received more cherished care because they seemed so lifelike after the very "wooden" faces of the wood dolls.

Wax Dolls Feel the Heat and Cold. The care of wax dolls is something few people think about. The very character of the material, becoming pliable at about 62°, would indicate the wisdom of keeping a wax doll away from any source of heat. Cold, however, can be quite as destructive, particularly for the wax-over-composition type. The thin wax coating becomes very brittle and will crack off when subjected to cold temperatures. The faces of so many old wax dolls are thus marred, not because of the vandalism of their first young owners, but rather because fond mamas packed them away in unheated attics or out in barns or carriage houses.

Modern doll artists using wax as a medium with which to create are few and far between, although a good many, at one time or another, have tried their hand at it. The time and skill required almost demands that the final product be confined to museums and/or special displays.

Poured wax is the method used by Gladys MacDowell and Lewis Sorensen. Heads are first modeled in clay from which a mold is made of either plaster of Paris or latex. Hands and sometimes complete torsos are done the same way. Melted wax is then cast in the molds. While it may be modified by various (usually secret) additives to gain strength, the finished product must be handled gently and kept out of direct sunlight.

During the 1950's, when the homemade Christmas Crèche was becoming so very popular, thousands of poured wax "babies," ranging from 1½ to 6 inches in size, were imported from Germany. These representations of the Christ Child were frequently turned into modern baby and child dolls by virtue of the styling of their clothes. They were always one piece productions and, despite modern clothes in which they may turn up, are easily recognizable by their pig-pink color. The smallest have molded hair. Some of the larger ones are endowed with overcurly startlingly blonde rayon tresses. During this same period molded wax heads of some beauty, designed for Christmas tree ornamentation, were imported from Austria. They may turn up in future years as parts of conventional dolls.

Wax is a very challenging material to work with. It can be carved or modeled as well as melted and poured. Beeswax may be bought from candle-making supply houses or local beekeepers.

PAPIER MÂCHÉ AND COMPOSITION DOLLS

In talking about wax dolls it was noted that one of the types was wax-over-composition. There are two classifications of dolls that came into being early in the nineteenth century—papier mâché and composition. The literal translation of papier mâché is "chewed paper" and this material, when wet, can be shaped and modeled as desired. When dried under heat it becomes hard and almost unbreakable. Composition, on the other hand, while manufactured into doll heads, bodies and parts just as papier mâché is

These 4-inch twins, c. 1830, have been preserved in pristine condition in a glass-fronted case. Beside each hangs a scallop-shell pincushion, a needlework item that became popular at a somewhat later date.

worked, consists of various materials mixed together to form the soft, plastic material required for modeling. All kinds of mixtures have been worked out and patented for "composition." One recipe includes sawdust, bran, glue and plaster of Paris.

The texture of composition heads made them a good base for coating with wax as it adhered rather well to the slightly rough surface. The features were painted on the composition in rather high colors before the wax was applied. Successive coats of wax served to soften and make more natural the vivid shades.

Both composition and papier mâché dolls were enameled to give a smooth skin-like texture. The features and eyes were painted on. Not all of these dolls had painted eyes, however, for with the mass production of glass eyes in Germany, it was relatively inexpensive to equip composition dolls with a handsome pair of eyes. Sometimes the eyes were stationary, others had "sleeping eyes." Many of the early composition dolls originated in Germany. These have beautiful blown glass eyes while other details of workmanship are quite fine.

WOOD AND BISQUE DOLLS

The Joel Ellis doll, left, reveals her characteristic booted legs. Right, the French bisque doll has pierced ears which dates her ten years later than the Ellis. Her legs are homemade replacements.

America's Earliest Doll Manufacturer. The first real doll manufacturer in America, Ludwig Greiner, patented a doll head in 1858. His patent was for the method of construction rather than for the material of which the head was made. Some authorities speak of "papier mâché Greiner's," while others say "composition Greiner's." To all intents and purposes, the terms are interchangeable. Papier mâché or composition, the important point at this moment is that the doll is not wood, or wax, or china, or any of the other material classifications. Composition dolls were made from the early 1800's right on up to today.

CHINA, BISQUE AND PARIAN DOLLS

China dolls are made of special clay that has been glazed and fired. The result is a doll having a very glossy smooth surface as contrasted with the delicately dull surface of bisque. The latter,

CHINA HEADED DOLLS

Three fine types of 19th century dolls illustrating distinctive hair styles and contemporary homemade dresses. About 1840-1860.

also, is a fired clay which has had no high glaze applied to it. The bisque doll more closely resembles the bloom of a beautiful human complexion than that of any other type of material used to make dolls. The Parian doll, another type of fired clay, is so called because it is supposed to resemble the exquisitely fine Parian marble. Porcelain, a still finer type of fired clay, was used for dolls, although its more prominent use was for figurines. Porcelain dolls are extremely rare and such examples of them that are in existence are quite lovely.

China dolls were almost entirely a German proposition. They were exported in ever growing numbers from the early 1800's up to World War I. They are among the commonest of dolls being offered by antique shops and dealers which testifies to the enormous quantities of them that were brought into this country. That they are numerous, however, does not mean that they are without interest to the collector. On the contrary, the variety of hair styles alone makes them an interesting group to search for.

Different Colors in China Dolls. There are various grades of china indicated by color. The dead white ones are the most common. Creamy white china is finer. Rarest of all is pink china, actually delicately flesh colored, and referred to by collectors and authorities as "pink luster." In no sense does the term "luster" as applied to dolls' heads mean what it does when used to designate a certain type of fine china used for dishes. In the latter case a pink luster teapot or cup is one in which the dominant color of the design is a real pink, to which an iridescent metal wash has been added to give the effect of gold.

The white china and creamy china doll appear with homemade as well as professionally made bodies of cloth or kid. They may or may not have china arms and legs. Some of the very fine kid bodies have kid arms and legs, with the fingers and toes indicated by stitching. Larger sized dolls have kid hands in which each finger is separate and distinct. When the doll obviously has original china legs, examine the feet or rather the shoe. If it is flat soled the doll probably dates before 1850. A shoe having a definite heel dates the doll (or the foot) after 1850.

Queen Victoria and the Blue-Eyed Dolls. One of the apocryphal stories about these dolls concerns their eyes. The vast majority of them have painted eyes and, for the most part, are blue. It is said that all dolls were made with brown eyes until the reign of Queen Victoria. Then, in compliment to her Majesty, dolls' eyes were made blue. It is a nice little story having no basis in fact. There are brown-eyed dolls made before, during and after Victoria's reign, although it is quite true that the number of blue-eyed ones far exceeded the brown. There were even a few gray-eyed dolls made. These are extremely rare. Another rather rare china doll is that having inset glass eyes.

Germans Capture French Bisque Dolls. The bisque doll, appearing in 1844 and growing in popularity with each successive year, usually had blown glass eyes. They were either stationary or "sleeping" and, with the characteristic skin-like appearance, contributed greatly to the realistically human effect. The bisque doll was developed and most exquisitely done in France. Every effort was made to make it the most beautiful doll in the world. Germany soon mastered the techniques and gradually forced the French manufacturers to give way to the inevitable. Soon the French bisque doll was being made almost exclusively in German factories.

Leather Dolls. A peculiarly American type, the rawhide leather doll head was patented in 1866 by Frank E. Darrow. Designed to be almost indestructible, the Darrow doll head was made by saturating the rawhide to make it pliable and elastic, then molding it in a die where steam pressure was applied to set and harden it. When completed, the head was painted by hand and did not look too different than the usual run of composition heads. Not many of them are in existence today, probably because rats have always loved rawhide and the Darrow dolls suffered accordingly. The doll was only manufactured for a short time, 1866 to 1877, because rodents quite literally ate up the business.

RUBBER AND CELLULOID

Dolls' heads were made of rubber as early as the 1840's. In 1851 heads appeared which were printed with the patent legend of Goodyear. These, like the composition heads, were an early attempt to make an unbreakable doll. Many of them were made in the same molds used for composition dolls, hence their similarity in style and hair-do. They soon became battered looking due to the cracking and peeling of the plant. The Goodyear patent mark on dolls refers only to the material used, not the manufacturer of the doll. The all-rubber doll was of much later dating.

The 20th century has seen great advances in the manufacturing of rubber dolls. They are to be found in all styles, textures and degrees of hardness. The most recent and attractive rubber doll to appear on the market is that modeled to look like an eight- or ten-year-old girl. Having a wig of human hair arranged simply and gracefully these well-dressed dolls are bound to become collectors' pieces in the future. However, it should be remembered that the modern rubber doll feels and looks vastly different from its older cousin.

The materials and methods involved in making celluloid were patented in 1869, although celluloid itself was first made in 1855. The first celluloid doll to be patented was dated 1881 but it is reasonable to suppose that, between 1869 and 1881, various dolls were manufactured from this interesting material. Its great virtue was its light weight. A basic skin color was included in the plastic but it had a tendency to fade. From 1881 on, various manufacturers here and in Germany experimented with celluloid dolls. Germany exported them in large quantities until the early 1930's. The older celluloid dolls have painted eyes and features, and modeled hair. Later examples show design advances such as inset glass eyes, set-in china teeth and pasted-on wigs.

RAG DOLLS

The oldest, as well as the youngest, dolls in history are the so-called rag dolls. They are so designated because, for the most part, they are made of fabric: face, body, arms, legs, hands and feet. A variety of materials have been used to stuff rag dolls, as well as

TWO CELLULOID DOLLS

The girl doll has inset glass eyes and a lovely wig. She is dressed in a period of considerabl[e] earlier date than the manufacturing date of the doll itself. The boy doll is in modern dres[s] and has molded hair. Both bear the tortoise trade mark and are from the collection [of] Mrs. Ralph Sandt, of the Sandt Doll Hospital, Easton, Pa.

other types of dolls. They include sawdust, bran, shredded or wadded rags, dried grasses, horsehair, crumpled paper, excelsior, cotton, wool, moss, in fact anything that was pliable or soft enough to be inserted into the cloth casing that gave shape to the doll. The oldest doll extant, made of strips of linen and stuffed with papyrus, dates back almost six thousand years. There are other dolls equally as old that are made of bone, wood, and carved ivory. They are indicative of the fact that dolls played a part in the early history of man.

Wide Variety of Types. From the very crude Egyptian doll of 4000 B.C. to the present day, rag dolls have been made by the average woman, professional seamstresses and world-renowned artists. They are a challenge to ingenuity and skill, but however crude the results, rag dolls have an endearing and enduring charm. Ranging in type from the simplest shape to the most sophisticated design, this kind of doll has a universal appeal. While largely the product of the unknown but skilled needle-woman, many rag dolls have been so beautifully or interestingly designed that their makers' names have become associated with them. That some of these dolls have been constructed on a skeleton of sorts and have a semi-hard construction or backing to the face and head does not change their classification. They are still rag dolls.

NOVELTY DOLLS

Into this extremely large group fall all those dolls that are made from a variety of materials originally designed for purposes other than doll making. For the most part, the classification refers to the construction of the head, although many novelty dolls are truly so because the entire doll is made of unusual materials. Among the novelty type heads are those made of:

> corncobs
> clay pipes
> rubber nipples
> wooden potato mashers

    wooden mixing spoons
    chestnuts, peanuts and walnuts
    dried apples and pears
    clothes pins
    twigs
    sponges
    shells
    wooden spools
    balls
    bone and ivory

The above materials are usually attached to a body of sorts. The styles of the bodies have an enormous range. Here are a few of the devices used in creating novelty dolls: Simple drapery used to give the effect of a torso and limbs; heads stuck on paper cones or in the necks of bottles; heads attached to a single stick with a short crosspiece of wood to simulate arms; heads sewed to stuffed rag bodies; and heads attached to really elaborate bodies which are constructed of wire skeletons covered with some soft material.

Entire dolls are also made of:

              corn husks
              birch bark
              maple and oak leaves
              sea shells
              sponge rubber
              pipe stem cleaners
              clothes pins
              spools
              adhesive tape
              peanuts

WHEN IS A "FIGURE" NOT A DOLL?

Real skill and ingenuity go into the creating and making of many of the novelty dolls. While the results are often interesting and effective, many of them should be classified as "figures" rather than as dolls. According to Webster's Unabridged Dictionary (and other leading dictionaries concur) the definition of doll is "an

RAG DOLLS

Here are two dolls from the comprehensive collection of the Doll Museum, Wenham, Mass. Doll at left is beautifully made and dressed in black silk. It is the thousandth doll made by a Southern artist specializing in this type. The "Merchant's Wife" above comes from Soviet Russia and, while using a fabric doll head and torso, is designed for a tea cosy. The expressiveness and modeling of face and hands are particularly good.

image in the form of a child, or sometimes an adult, for the amusement of little girls." Do you doubt that it is frequently true of big girls too?

As applied to collecting, the term doll is, I believe, too loosely and generally used. Many of the large and famous doll collections contain great numbers of items that should be more correctly classed as figures. Never designed as playthings or toys but created rather as a demonstration of artistic skill, or an ingenious use of odd materials, or for these very specific purposes: plays (marionettes and puppets), religious symbols (crèche and nativity groups, ancestor images, totems and voodoos), miniature decorative objects (sea shell figures, figures made from native flora, etc.), such facsimiles (reasonable or otherwise) of the human figure as belong in a separate and distinct class by themselves. Since there is no clear, distinct and generally accepted rule of classification, your collecting is controlled only by your own discrimination, tastes and desires.

WHAT KIND OF DOLLS SHALL WE COLLECT?

The business of collecting dolls, and it really is big business, can be more absorbing than you ever dreamed of. Since the field is so varied and complex it is a good idea to start slowly and really have some sort of a plan in mind. Many collectors concentrate on one or two types: bisque heads and Penny Woodens, various kinds of kid bodies, foreign costume dolls, or portrait dolls. The possibilities are almost unlimited when you consider not only the tremendous number of styles from which to select but also the equally fascinating factors of hair styles, sizes and the infinite variety of materials. Then, of course, there are the "name dolls," those bearing patent names, manufacturer's or designer's names and historical names.

Money-Raising Dolls. There are "Benefit" dolls, designed for the specific purpose of raising money for charitable causes. During the Civil War many dolls were costumed and sold at rallies to raise money for the Sanitary Commission or Red Cross. Many of them are now owned by private collectors. Every now and then one of

BENEFIT DOLLS

They usually can be dated rather accurately.
The man doll at left was made to sell at a fair for
raising money for the Bunker Hill Monument.
The Liberty doll above was used for raising
funds for the Sanitary Commission of the Civil
War, 1864-65. She was used as a door-stop, having lower part filled with sand.

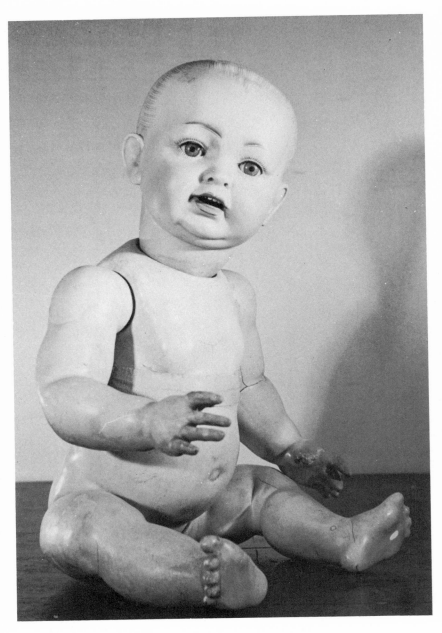

20TH CENTURY BABY DOLL

Made about 1905, this fine, realistically modeled baby doll with composition
body and bisque head has a voice box in its chest. When tilted forward it bleats
"Ma-ma." Its beautifully detailed handmade clothes were inherited from a real
six month old baby. It is probably American made.

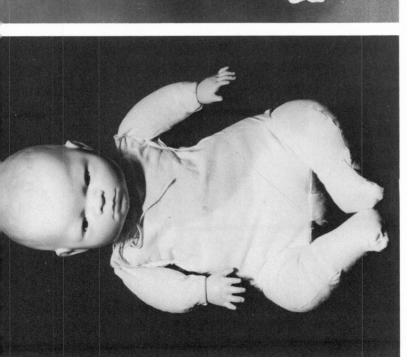

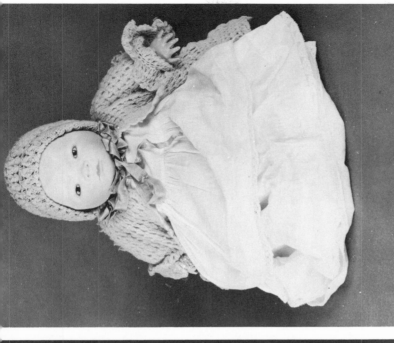

THE EVER POPULAR BYE-LO BABY

Modeled by Grace Storey Putnam after a four day old infant, its bisque head and composition hands were manufactured in Germany. Called the "Million Dollar Baby," it was manufactured from 1920 to 1944. A new issue was advertised in 1968. The first 200 Bye-Los had wax heads, then bisque, then composition.

these Civil War dolls turns up for sale. Following the Civil War dolls, one finds various dolls produced during and after World War I that were also created for the benefit of war victims.

The Paderewski dolls, designed and made by Polish artists, were sold in New York and Paris for Polish Relief. Somewhat later, a group of White Russians designed and made a series of dolls dressed in the costumes of old Russia. Barbaric splendor rather than beauty characterized these dolls. The proceeds from their sale went to the relief of needy White Russians, both in New York and Paris. Today one is likely to find these dolls in rummage sales or thrift shops. They have been discarded because the material used for their faces and hands (chiffon or extremely sheer silk stockings) has disintegrated. It is not difficult to restore the faces and hands. They are worth looking for because of their fine costumes.

Dolls in World War II. World War II has produced some Benefit dolls. Made by displaced persons in various European camps, they are interesting because they demonstrate so clearly the ingenuity and talents of their creators. Made of scraps and bits of materials, they contribute their part to the emotional and spiritual rehabilitation as well as to the financial gain. A few quite beautifully costumed dolls are now coming from Italy. Exquisite workmanship and lovely fabrics characterize these dolls which are sold for Italian Post-War Relief. They are quite expensive but the beauty of their costumes is worth the price.

In Your Own Neighborhood. Dolls have been used, through exhibitions, lotteries and rallies, to raise money for other purposes besides war relief. Usually of a local nature, the dolls so used were less publicized and often forgotten. It would be interesting to talk to the older residents about the possibility of such events having taken place in a community. It just requires a few pointed questions to unearth some valuable information which may lead to an addition to your collection, or to an interesting story about a local doll celebrity.

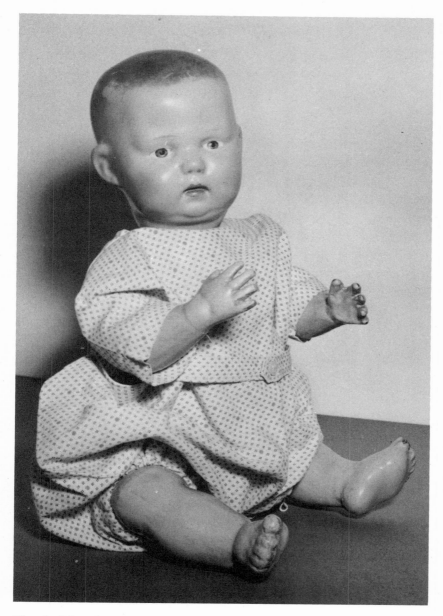

The A. Schoenhut Co. of Philadelphia manufactured this wood boy baby in 1915. He is 14 inches high and dressed in a typical "romper" of the period. Arms and legs are movable at shoulders and hips. Less "pretty" than the bisque head baby dolls of the period, he took more loving abuse. While he was almost unbreakable, his skin was subject to cracking and chipping.

Among the Schoenhut specialities was this "Manikin," a fully articulated wood doll dressed as a football player in 1915. Like the famous circus figures made by Schoenhut, he was designed for boys and might be considered the prototype of the excellent "G. I. Joe" series of composition dolls that came onto the market in the late 1960's.

STORY BOOK, PORTRAIT AND COSTUME DOLLS

This group is as wide in scope and as varied in interest as one could possibly desire. Starting back in the 1830's and continuing through to the present day, portrait dolls include almost every well known or historical personage who captured popular fancy. Queen Victoria, while no beauty, had instant appeal because of her extreme youth and extraordinarily powerful position as Queen of England. Many dolls purporting to be portraits of Victoria appeared during the early years of her reign. Jenny Lind, "the Swedish Nightingale," was also the subject of various portrait dolls. Alice in Wonderland has appeared in many types of dolls, the earliest being a china-headed one that is a fair facsimile of the famous Tenniel illustration. Fairy stories have contributed their characters to doll portrait creations as have early funny-paper characters like Buster Brown, Palmer Cox's Brownies, and various cereal companies' trade-marked characters like Aunt Jemima and Rastus.

Think Before You Make Your Selection. With a classification as tremendous as this one, including as it does a wealth of styles and types of materials, the amateur collector would do well to make progress slowly. Costume dolls alone could make a tremendous collection. With the popularity of world travel developed and promoted during the period between World Wars I and II, the growth of foreign costume dolls was enormous. Designed almost exclusively for the tourist trade, they are for the most part cheaply made and poorly, although colorfully, dressed. Not all of them, however, could be so criticized.

Watch for Quality. There have always been available to the discriminating customer foreign costume dolls of great beauty and distinction. Many of these really fine examples turn up for sale and they are well worth waiting for. Particularly interesting are the older (made prior to World War I) costume dolls, as they are truly representative of the countries from which they came. Contemporary fabrics, embroideries and laces used for their clothes document their authenticity. More modern costume dolls, both domestic and foreign, frequently sacrifice authenticity and strive for effect rather than accurate detail.

More Doll Types Which Everybody Likes. Baby dolls, doll-house dolls, novelty dolls, dolls of specific sizes (usually scaled in miniature such as six or four inches and under), boy dolls, brown-eyed dolls, folk lore dolls, character and regional dolls—the list is legion and completely a matter of personal choice. Who is to say that one collection is more interesting than another? It is so completely a personal matter that you, and you alone, write the rules controlling it.

WHAT ABOUT MARKET PRICES?

Whether or not your collection is a valuable one in a purely monetary sense depends upon your knowledge, astuteness and, too frequently, the ability to outbid another collector. There are certain standards and values attached to specific types and styles of dolls. To some extent they control the market prices. On the other hand, the rapid growth of doll collecting means that in many cases prices are gauged according to what the traffic will bear. In fairness to yourself, as well as to other amateur collectors, you should become familiar with doll jargon as well as with current doll prices.

How Much Should a Good Doll Cost? That depends entirely upon what constitutes a good doll. Because a doll is old does not necessarily mean that it is valuable. This country was flooded with china-head dolls from Germany all during the last century and as late as the twenties in this century. Thousands of bisque heads were brought in, many of them quite common, while some are of great beauty and fineness. Which is the more valuable? Workmanship and artistry are usually to be preferred above mere age especially when the difference is relatively slight. Association and history, when authenticated, immediately control the price of a doll. Since there are relatively few genuine examples extant and since most of those examples are owned by museums or are in im-

OUT FOR A STROLL
A group of doll-house dolls, dated 1890, from the Sandt Doll Hospital Collection.

portant private collections, their cost is of little interest to the average collector. Important collections seldom come up for public sale except in the event of death of the collector. By the time you find out about it, unless it occurs in your own community, the prizes will have been snatched up by other important collectors who have probably been waiting for years for just such an opportunity.

Beware of Ridiculous Prices. "Name" dolls (those bearing the manufacturer's name, trademark or patent registration), again are subject to market fluctuations. Not all the dolls of one brand name are equal in value despite the fact that they may have all originated within a year or two of each other. Another factor that qualifies price is that of the "all original" doll against the reconstructed or redressed doll. This factor is discussed later on in the section devoted to determining the age of dolls. Popularity of a certain type accounts for a price rise or apparent high price. This, together with the lack of knowledge on the part of both many a shopkeeper and the amateur collector, is responsible for the fancy and often ridiculous prices of some dolls.

COMPARE LIST PRICES

One of the best ways to find out about doll prices and to determine just what is fair to pay is by comparing prices in local shops with prices on the doll lists from reliable and well known doll houses. A great deal of the doll business is done by mail and the better houses send out lists at frequent intervals to advise customers of new items and rare and interesting examples. Frequently, it is far better to buy from these houses than from local shops unless, of course, your knowledge is such that you are not likely to be fooled. That does not mean that every shopkeeper selling dolls is not to be trusted. Far from it. It does mean that many shopkeepers, jumping on this new and interesting bandwagon, know very little more, if as much as *you* do about dolls. Their business is to sell. It is your business to know what you are buying and to guard yourself against inaccurate, if enthusiastic and interesting, sales talk.

Lists of mail-order doll firms may be obtained from the advertisements in *Hobbies* magazine. Many of these houses supply for a small charge actual photographs of the dolls for your examination. These, together with price lists, should give you a fair picture of the current market.

SIZE OR MONEY VALUE DOES NOT MAKE A GOOD COLLECTION

One last word about collecting. Even though so many of the collections are made up of old and antique dolls, this is no valid reason for your trying to duplicate the same sort of thing. We are too prone to attach an almost exclusive monetary value to our possessions, or to think our collections are significant if their items are large in number. Too often such large collections consist of a hodgepodge of items gathered without discrimination, simply to satisfy an acquisitive instinct.

Personal Significance. A really valuable collection can be quite small but so perfect in its way that it is of necessity limited. For instance, one woman is gradually putting a collection together that

A STORY BOOK GROUP

This delightful group by Florence Bradshaw Brown shows Mary, her lamb, and two school-mates. Dolls are built on wire frames and have molded faces covered with kidskin.

has great personal significance at the moment and will, if kept intact, grow in monetary value as the years go on. Beginning with the infancy of her daughter, this mother purchased a baby doll and dressed it in an exact replica of her baby's christening gown. As the child grew older and important events occurred, other dolls representing similar age levels, were again dressed in miniature duplicates of the child's clothes. Today there are some fifteen dolls in this collection covering the christening, the first birthday, the first Christmas, the first day at school, the camp uniform, the Girl

Scout uniform, the costume worn in the first school play, etc.

As a history of the high points of a child's life the intrinsic value of such a collection is enormous. As a record of the change in children's fashions this collection will increase in monetary value as the years go on. To authenticate this collection, the mother should document each doll with the full name of the child, the date and event for which it was made. Written cards and paper labels have a way of becoming detached and lost. For a permanent record, such information should be written with waterproof ink on a small piece of fine, sheer material, which is then sewn inside the clothes.

Specialized Collections. Another specialized and extremely interesting collection is that of a group of dolls authentically costumed in the habits of the various orders of Catholic Nuns. Individual dolls were sent to the mother house of each order to be costumed there. In this way each nun-doll is absolutely authentic and accurate to the tiniest detail. The dolls used are modern bisque-headed ones.

Yes, collecting is fun but since it does take time and some investment, make your collecting profitable from every angle. Let it express yourself, your interests, and your ever increasing knowledge.

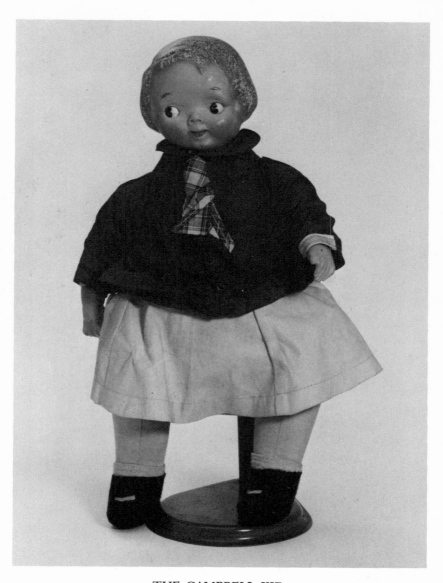

THE CAMPBELL KID

This early 20th century German made doll was inspired by the illustrations in
the advertisements of a soup company. Head and hands are composition and the
body cloth. Never quite as popular as the Kewpies (also born of illustrations by
their creator Rose O'Neill before being manufactured as dolls), Campbell Kids
are worth a place in any doll collection. They were always labeled although the
labels, more often than not, were taken off by their young owners. Their distinguishing characteristic was the perfectly round eyes and enormous irises
which were always turned sideways.

Rare Queen Anne dolls made prior to 1750.
Both have human hair and inset glass eyes.
Their original clothes are rich and beautifully detailed; the man is in court dress of
red satin with gold braid trim and buttons
and the woman in a lace trimmed brocade
"morning gown" with a fine linen apron
and cap.

9.

Old Dolls

*W*HEN A DOLL HAS BEEN HANDED DOWN IN ONE FAMILY
and its history is clear cut and indisputable, it is quite probable
that the date attached to its origin is the correct one.

When a doll is labeled with the manufacturer's or designer's
name, it is relatively easy to attach a logical and probably accurate
date to it, if the date itself is not included in the marking or label.

When a doll is documented in some way by personal letter, by
family or individual portrait, daguerreotype or photograph in
which the doll is included, this accurate dating is quite simple.

It is rather easy to check back on dates when a doll has any
particularly significant personal association, such as: "Given to
Aunt Mary when she was two years old by Mr. Harold Jamieson,
founder of the Anoka News"; "Treasured by my grandmother
who carried it across the plains in a covered wagon"; "Bequeathed
to my oldest sister by Mrs. William Bates who bought it in Paris
on her wedding trip."

Some old dolls have this pertinent and desirable information

POLLY SUMNER

Here is a wooden doll, who came to this country on Dec. 16, 1773, aboard the ship that gave rise to the Boston Tea Party. Her head is painted and has glass eyes. She is owned by the Bostonian Society.

written on the body or the shoulder-head of the doll, but most other methods of dating dolls are problematical and debatable.

DETECTING OF DOLL DATES

By a process of elimination and deduction it is possible to arrive at an acceptable, if not accurate, date for the doll.

It is extremely easy to tell whether the entire doll (body, arms, legs, head) is professionally made. Just as simply as you can spot a homemade dress from a "store-bought" one, so you can spot the doll body made by the amateur. Up until about 1855, all doll bodies were handmade. Elias Howe invented the sewing machine in 1846. By the end of 1847 there were only ten sewing machines in the entire country! Manufacturing them was a slow and complicated job, consequently production was anything but rapid. The machine-stitched doll body was not the general rule until late in the 1850's. Even then, the professionally handsewn doll body continued for some time into the next decade.

Right: A QUAKER DOLL

Dressed by Mrs. Sara Rutter of Philadelphia in 1825, this doll illustrates the type of costume worn by the Friends at that date of gray taffeta with a close fitting bodice. Neckline is softened with a pleated linen frill. The fine white shawl is typical.

Below: A WAX FASHION DOLL

This doll was presented to Sarah Duffield of Philadelphia in 1766 by Mrs. John Penn, wife of the last Colonial Governor of the Province of Pennsylvania. She is 9 inches tall and dressed in red crossbar on white taffeta over a hooped petticoat of same material. The apron, worn under the stomacher, is of soft green silk. All flounces have pinked edges. Hair was originally powdered and curled in the French fashion of the time. Her French slippers are high heeled. She wears a bracelet and necklace.

FACTS ARE HIDDEN IN DETAILS

The feet and legs of a doll, when they match the material of the head, roughly indicate age. If the modeled-on shoe is heelless or flat soled, the chances are very good that it dates prior to the 1860's. Beware, however, of accepting this as conclusive evidence. It is wise to remember that doll manufacturers did not discard old molds until they were worn out, consequently a doll made in 1868–69 could still have the old style shoe.

Learn About Part Replacements. It was not uncommon to replace a lost leg on a new doll with a leg taken from an old doll. This is frequently done today in the "restoring" of old dolls only in reverse; i. e., the "restored" leg is much more apt to be of a later date than the head of the doll. The reliable dealer will point this fact out to a prospective customer. The uniniated dealer may not even know that such a replacement exists. Look for yourself. Examine the joinings of legs and arms. You can tell whether the limb is a replacement or original by the condition and type of stitching of the joining. The cloth used for the upper legs and arms is also a dead give-away. Does it match the body?

If the clothes of the doll are supposed to be original, check fashion points against listings in later pages. Also check hand-sewing, machine or hand embroidery, as well as other trimmings and types of materials.

STYLE OF HAIR-DO REVEALS DATES

A common way to arrive at the approximate age of a doll is by studying the hair-do. On the face of things this seems logical. We know from old prints, old magazines, portraits and pictures, that certain ways of doing the hair were popular during specific periods. It is also known that the mold from which a doll was made was used over and over. The life of a mold may have extended any time between six months and a number of years. If the model proved popular, the mold was duplicated exactly. Thus a certain hair-do, supposedly characteristic of a short period, might be per-

THREE PENNY WOODENS

These are wooden dolls from the Doll Museum, Wenham, Mass. Center doll illustrates styling of body and form of articulating the limbs. Her companions show the elaborate costuming given these tiny ones. As contrasted with the Penny Woodens on page 126, these have been dressed by an expert needlewoman with a highly developed fashion sense. Early 1830's.

petuated over many years in doll heads. This is a point to keep in mind when examining china, papier mâché and composition heads.

One style of hair-do that leaves little doubt as to its exact period is that seen on wooden dolls of the 1828–1838 period. It is a grotesque style. Large puffs or groups of curls are posed above the ears. The back and top of head are quite flat, then a weird arrangement of hair soars into the air like a fanciful chimney. This edifice was usually accomplished by the use of plaster or composition added to the wooden head. In its day it was called "Apollo's Knot" and was frequently embellished with flowers and ribbon loops.

AGE TOLD BY SHOULDER CURVE

Another way of determining the approximate age of a shoulder-head is by examining the neck and shoulder line. If a graceful reverse curve sweeps down from tip of ear to bottom of shoulder piece and if the slope of the shoulder is deep rather than broad,

This professionally made French wooden doll of the Empire Period (c. 1820) has the typical plaster coating on arms and shoulder-head. The top-knot was also of plaster. While it is doubtful that the gown is original, its styling is completely authentic for the period, as are the ballet-type slippers and characteristic shawl. She is on display at the Essex Institute, Salem, Mass.

the doll is early or mid-nineteenth century. As fashions in clothes changed, bringing the neckline of daytime gowns closer and closer to the throat, the necessity for the deep shoulder line was eliminated. It is also true that as the century progressed the fashionable shoulder line for women became somewhat broader. This mode was, of course, picked up by doll manufacturers, for it meant considerable saving in both weight and amount of material in making the shoulder-head.

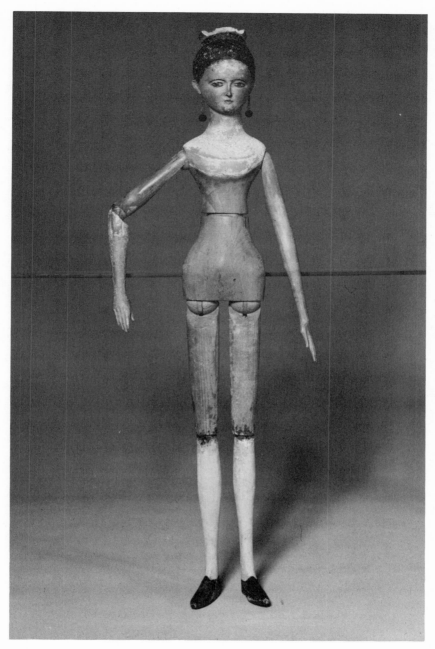

Although made in Austria during the Empire Period, this 34 inch wooden doll is a first cousin to the French one on the opposite page. Both dolls are identically articulated and both have characteristic small mouths, thin, well-defined noses and large painted eyes. The earrings, very mid-20th century in design, were put on the doll when she was made. Her flat, black painted slippers probably indicate that she was dressed for the street.

This composition headed doll dressed as a Quaker lady of the 1830's may have been used as a door-stop or simply as a decorative piece for a bureau or shelf. Under her tattered gray taffeta gown may be seen the stuffed cylinder that makes this theory tenable. Her bonnet and soft white sheer muslin fichu are authentic style details of the period.

COMPARING MODELS OF DIFFERENT TIMES

Does the head of the doll turn (swivel-neck)? Prior to 1861 there are no authenticated dolls with swivel-necks.

Penny Wooden peg-jointed dolls are particularly hard to place accurately. Made over a period of some two hundred years with little or no change in detail or finish, the Penny Woodens might be dated any time. It is natural, since we have been conditioned to thinking that the older the doll the more valuable it is, to set the date of a Penny Wooden at a much earlier figure than it probably could be. I have a four-inch Penny Wooden documented as having been bought in 1842. A collector friend also has a Penny Wooden of the same size which she claims (without tangible support) to be dated about 1770. When the two dolls were laid on a table side by side, only the spot of cement on the sole of my doll served to distinguish it from its great-great-grandmother.

Glass eyes are no indication of age, as they were used in dolls and small religious figures for centuries. The "sleeping eyes" are a nineteenth century product. Those that open and shut by means of a wire to be pushed up and down (wire protruded from side of doll) or by pulling a string, appeared as early as the 1820's. The "sleeping eyes" that worked automatically by means of an inner counter weight appeared in the late 1820's and, with improvements, has continued in use to the present day.

At this point you may well ask just exactly how you can determine the exact age of a doll when it has no positive authentication, documentation, printed or embossed trade name. The truthful answer is—it is next to impossible to *exactly* date such a doll! An approximate date, indicated by the word *circa*, Latin for "about," may be given, but not an exact and specific date.

WHAT IS THE IMPORTANCE OF A DATE?

The importance of an exact date depends upon the point of view involved on the part of the collector. The attractiveness of the dolls is infinitely greater than a matter of dating. So many other important factors enter the picture that are of equal or greater consequence to the average person. Beauty or homeliness, charm, character, workmanship, clothes, association or history, an indefinable something that appeals to you alone—all are potent influences that counter balance the disputable point of a date.

Knowledge Lends Appreciation. Naturally, it is foolish to completely disregard the age of a doll. Knowing its approximate period adds to the appreciation of the doll itself. The more one learns about various periods of the past, the keener becomes one's interest and ability to recognize and appreciate various types of dolls. While keeping in mind the points discussed, make objective comparisons with dolls of known dates. Place them side by side, if possible. Compare them from every angle. The discussion of their points will teach you more than it is possible to learn from words and pictures alone.

19TH CENTURY FASHION POINTS REVEAL CLUES TO DATING

There are certain well defined and authentic fashion details that are characteristic of the 19th century. These details are important in the recognition of the probable age of those dolls which wear their original clothes because doll wardrobes were exact duplicates in miniature of current fashions. Even homemade doll costumes closely followed the styles worn by adults.

You will find below the fashion highpoints of the nineteenth century. Space does not allow a really full and detailed description of individual styles. These may be ascertained by reference to contemporary paintings and illustrations for various books, *Godey's Ladies' Books*, as well as other fashion periodicals and books on costume design.

HOOPSKIRTS: Introduced in Paris in 1839; appeared in U. S. in 1840. The use of a frame to distend skirts had disappeared by 1780. Petticoats served the purpose. The hoopskirt as we know it—a series of wire circles that became progressively larger towards the bottom—was not generally worn in this country until the mid-1840's. American manufacturers improved the design to such an extent that it became known in England and Europe as the "cage américaine."

ENGLISH PEDLAR DOLL

Pedlar dolls were made both in England and in America usually by professional doll makers but often by the home doll maker. In the latter case they had commercially made heads and hands. Their original interest and their value to today's collector lies in the tray or basket these dolls carry, filled with up to a hundred miniature items representing the items actual women pedlars carried walking from village to village to sell their wares.

TWO WOOD DOLLS

They are dated about 1820 and are stylishly dressed.

Leonide, a fashionable lady of the 1870's, is 15 inches tall, has a bisque head, kid hands and arms and cloth body, legs and feet. Her walking costume was the height of fashion as was the blue satin bow on top of her French poodle's head. Her gowns were so perfectly made and marvelously detailed that they served as fashion models for a leading dressmaker in Salem, Mass., although Leonide was brought there from Paris as a gift to a

As well as the evening gowns, morning gowns, walking and traveling suits, Leonide's trunk contained undergarments and an assortment of fashion accessories and trinkets every well dressed lady of that period had to have.

SHORT HAIR: for grown women, 1798–1805 and again in the early 1890's.

ONE-PIECE GOWNS: 1798–1810. Very low cut over breasts. Waistline indicated by cord or ribbon tied tightly directly below breasts. Gown fell in perfectly straight narrow line to feet. Short, tight sleeve, or tiny cap sleeve. Light sheer cottons. No underclothes. About 1805, an overgarment was added which was cut in front to show gown beneath, or cut in form of tunic.

BONNETS: known as early as 1797. Common by 1805. Grew progressively larger to form the "poke bonnet" of the 1830–40 period, then diminished in size to the wee affairs worn on back of head in 1860's.

SHAWLS: the rage by 1810. Continued in popularity, and made of many different materials, up until the 1880's.

CORSETS: appeared in 1809, common by 1830. Continued throughout rest of century.

SLIPPERS: 1798–1850's; soft, heelless, made of satin for evening wear, somewhat pointed of toe until about 1835, then rather square-toed. Dancing slippers similar to modern ballet slippers. Daytime slippers were cut somewhat higher and laced over instep (see sketch on page 230 of French boot made in 1849). By 1860, low heels and sturdier construction of "shoe" were common.

UNDERDRAWERS: 1820 but not universal until the 1830's. Long, tight fitting, lace trimmed. Called "pantalettes."

TURBANS: 1810–1830. Rich materials or figured gauzes, trimmed with jewels and plumes. For matrons. Young girls wore wreaths of flowers in hair.

MITTS: black silk, fingerless, appeared about 1830. Very popular by 1840.

CURLS: worn drawn up high on head, large ones supported by wire frames on top of head. By 1840 curls and ringlets began to be worn falling to neck or shoulder, loose or clustered.

RIBBONS: 1820. To trim bottom of skirts, in form of bows, bands and loops. By 1840, extensively used as trim on bodices.

RUFFLES: of self-material and rather narrow, used well below knee line on the bell bottomed skirts of the 1820's. Continued in this form, while appearing on sleeves and bodices as well as edging shawls and scarves, through the 1870's.

FLOUNCES: really a ruffle that was eight or more inches wide; appeared in the early 1840's. Flounces grew in size and moved up to the waistline. In this form, by 1850, they were really two-or-three-tiered skirts, for daytime; many-flounced skirts for evening wear. When made of, or trimmed with, lace or fringe or ribbon or braid, flounces were known as "volants."

SNOODS: 1858–1870. Nets made of cord, ribbon or strung pearls, used to confine the hair at back of head and nape of neck. Elaborately trimmed for evening.

CHIGNONS: 1860–1870. Large, heavy knot of hair worn at nape of neck, often held by a net or snood. The hair was flat on top of head and drawn down smoothly to knot.

CRINOLINE: a stiffening fabric used to distend women's skirts. The word is used interchangeably with "hoopskirts." Its use in fashion disappeared by 1870 when skirts assumed the characteristic bunched-up-in-back look which not only evolved into the bustle, but stayed in fashion for about twenty years.

BUSTLE: by 1870, the popularity of elaborate underskirts resulted in pulling up and fastening the overskirt to display them. The trend towards pushing the fullness of the drawn-up overskirt towards the back developed the use of a pad of stiffening, tied on the waist and hanging over the buttocks, to support and further distend the bunched-up-in-back overskirt.

BODICES: from 1815 to 1890, all bodices were extremely tight. Their length varied from just below the breasts, to the normal waistline, to the long molded line of the 1880's which had no defined waistline. Accent was always on the tiny waist, the youthful breastline. Trimming ranged from complete simplicity to the most extravagant elaboration but the basic bodice was held tight and snug usually by means of a form-fitting lining. The appearance of the shirtwaist in the 1890's was the first break away from the fitted bodice.

Marie, another French doll of the 1870's, was bought in Paris and brought to Mary Crowninshield Endicott of Salem by a friend of her mother's. Her head and hands are bisque, feet and legs composition. Her body, white kid over jointed wood, would indicate that she is an early Jumeau. Her wardrobe included an astonishing number of hats and accessories: about 75 items and all of them of the finest materials and workmanship.

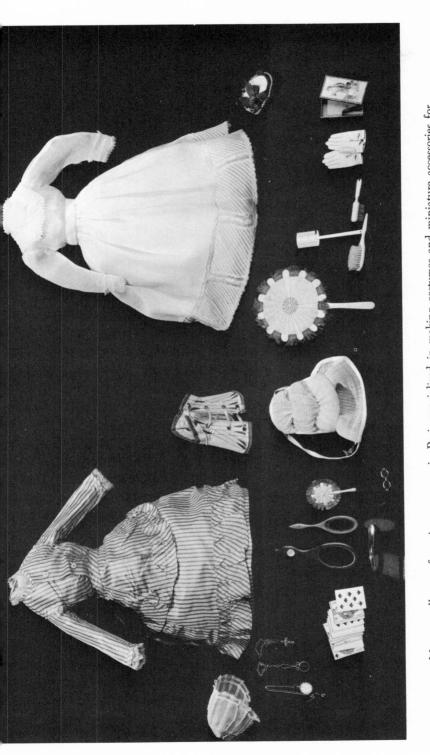

Many small manufacturing concerns in Paris specialized in making costumes and miniature accessories for dolls such as those shown here that are part of Marie's wardrobe. Gloves, jewelry (real gold and silver and often set with tiny but authentic precious stones), lorgnettes, eyeglasses and opera glasses, handbags, hats, shoes, undergarments and corsets, stockings, fans and toilet articles were made with same precision and care as were those made for the women who bought these tiny treasures.

BALL GOWNS: until the influence of the Empress Eugenie (1853), ball gowns were predominantly white. Soft, delicate pastels were used but the white gown was most popular, especially for young girls. Bodices were very tight, off-shoulder, often sleeveless or with tiny cap sleeves. Skirts followed current trends in silhouette, but were much more elaborately trimmed with lace, ribbons, embroideries, clusters of flowers or puffs. Fabrics: tulle, net, gauze, tarlatan, crepe and sheer cottons like batiste and muslin. By 1855, Eugenie had introduced the fashion of more violent colors for evening and daytime, and velvet trimming was seen on practically everything. French fashions, then as now, influenced the civilized world, styles introduced by the Empress Eugenie serving to strengthen their ascendancy, even in the world of dolls.

SKIRTS: 1798–1810. Straight and narrow, falling from directly below the breasts.

By 1815, some fullness was being introduced, mainly at the back. Waistline still abnormally high.

By 1820, the bell bottomed skirt was popular. Falling from the high waistline in a straight line, its hem was distended by means of ruffles, ribbon trim, stuffed rolls of self-fabric (called rouleaux), ruching or other forms of trimming.

By 1830, the waistline had descended to the normal point and skirts were becoming very much fuller. During the 30's, the skirts were held out by as many as six petticoats. The invention of the hoopskirt (1839) or crinoline removed the necessity of so many petticoats.

Skirts became progressively fuller, reaching their peak by the mid 60's.

By 1870, the bunched-up-in-back look began to appear with a progressive diminishing in size of the underskirt.

By 1880, the long, molded, form-fitting line from neck to knee, with fullness and most decoration concentrated at the back.

By 1890, waistlines were abnormally small, although the general silhouette otherwise closely approximated that of the 1830's. Skirts swept the ground and sleeves were extraordinarily distended.

SLEEVES: 1800–1815. Short and narrow or short and slightly puffed.

1820. Long and loosely form-fitting or long and wide at bottom caught by a tight band or ribbon at wrist.

1830. Beginning of real elaboration in sleeves which became mammoth in size by the 1840's, then slimmed down again to more normal proportions.

1850. Three-quarter bell sleeves to display a series of dainty and delicately elaborate undersleeves, usually white, the lowest one of which was caught in to wrist by band or narrow cuff. These sleeves were called "Pagodas."

1860–70. Fairly simple, following natural shape of arm. Restrained trimming of braid, ribbon, lace or narrow Val ruffles, confined to bottom of sleeve.

1875. Top puffs and ruffles began to adorn the otherwise simple sleeve.

1888 through the 90's. Revival of enormous and elaborate sleeves of the 30's. Then, slight simplification developing into the characteristic leg-of-mutton sleeve.

AUTHENTIC FASHION DETAILS OF THE
1830–1850 PERIOD

On the following page are a number of dressmaking details taken from a seamstress's guide book published during the second quarter of the 19th century. They are shown here for the guidance of the doll dressmaker who is interested not only in achieving variety in the styles of garments she wishes to make, but also as a guide in duplicating authentic fashion points. Naturally, the size of the patterns must be adjusted to the specific doll. This is best done by first cutting them in tissue paper, making necessary adjustments, then cutting the fabric from the perfected master pattern.

1. Basic bodice. This style was designed to be finely pleated, tucked or shirred to body-fitting size. The neckline was finished with narrow bias self-binding. In width, the neck extended just far enough out to keep it from slipping off the shoulders. The back, A, is cut in two pieces. The front, B, is

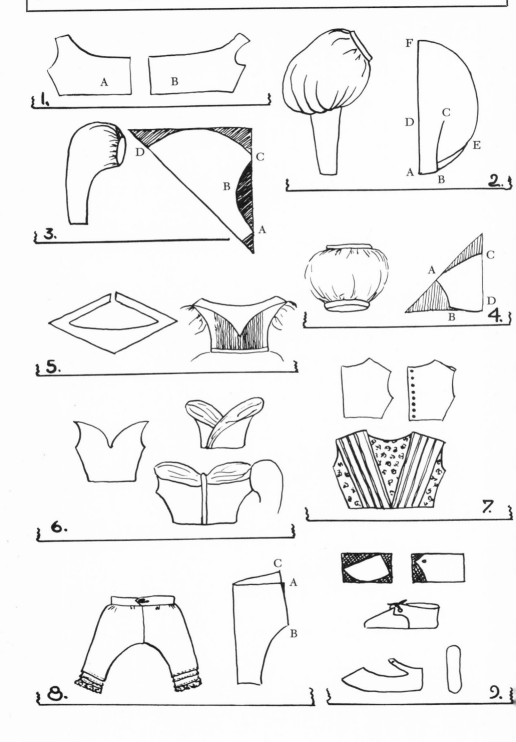

cut in one piece of doubled material, having the fold line at center front.

2. A popular sleeve of the 30's, later revived in the 90's. A circle is folded in half with the foldline indicated along A-D-F of sketch. Cut along B-C. Shorten front curve as shown. Stitch B-C to make lower arm part of sleeve. Stitch from F to E. Shorter front curve is picked up and gathered to line D-C. Longer back curve is done same way on back of sleeve.

3. Full top sleeve, forerunner of the leg-of-mutton. Fold a square diagonally as shown and cut out shaded areas. The line A-B-C is stitched together. The line C-D is gathered to fit armhole.

4. A charming short puffed sleeve. Cut as shown on doubled fabric. The line A-B is seamed together. A-C is shirred into armhole, B-D shirred into narrow bias band of size to fit arm.

5. Contrasting trim on bodice. Cut as shown and stitched down to pin tucked bodice. Looped braid or narrow lace ruffle outlines the trimming piece.

6. A smooth bodice adorned with bias folds of self material.

7. A morning frock bodice with tucked contrasting bands stitched down both back and front.

8. Underdrawers, trimmed with tucks and lace ruffles. Notice that line A-B indicates front. Line A-C is back, thus giving necessary room through seat. Top is gathered into waistband.

9. Slippers.

SHOE AND BONNET TAKEN FROM A SWISS WAX DOLL, 1849

The patterns shown on the following page are of actual size to fit a Swiss wax doll that was bought in Paris in 1849. The doll is 30 inches tall and endowed with human hair inserted into wax head. Her pink cotton dress had a bodice with bias folds placed lower down, starting at the lower armholes and crossing the breast.

PATTERN FOR FRENCH BONNET AND SLIPPER

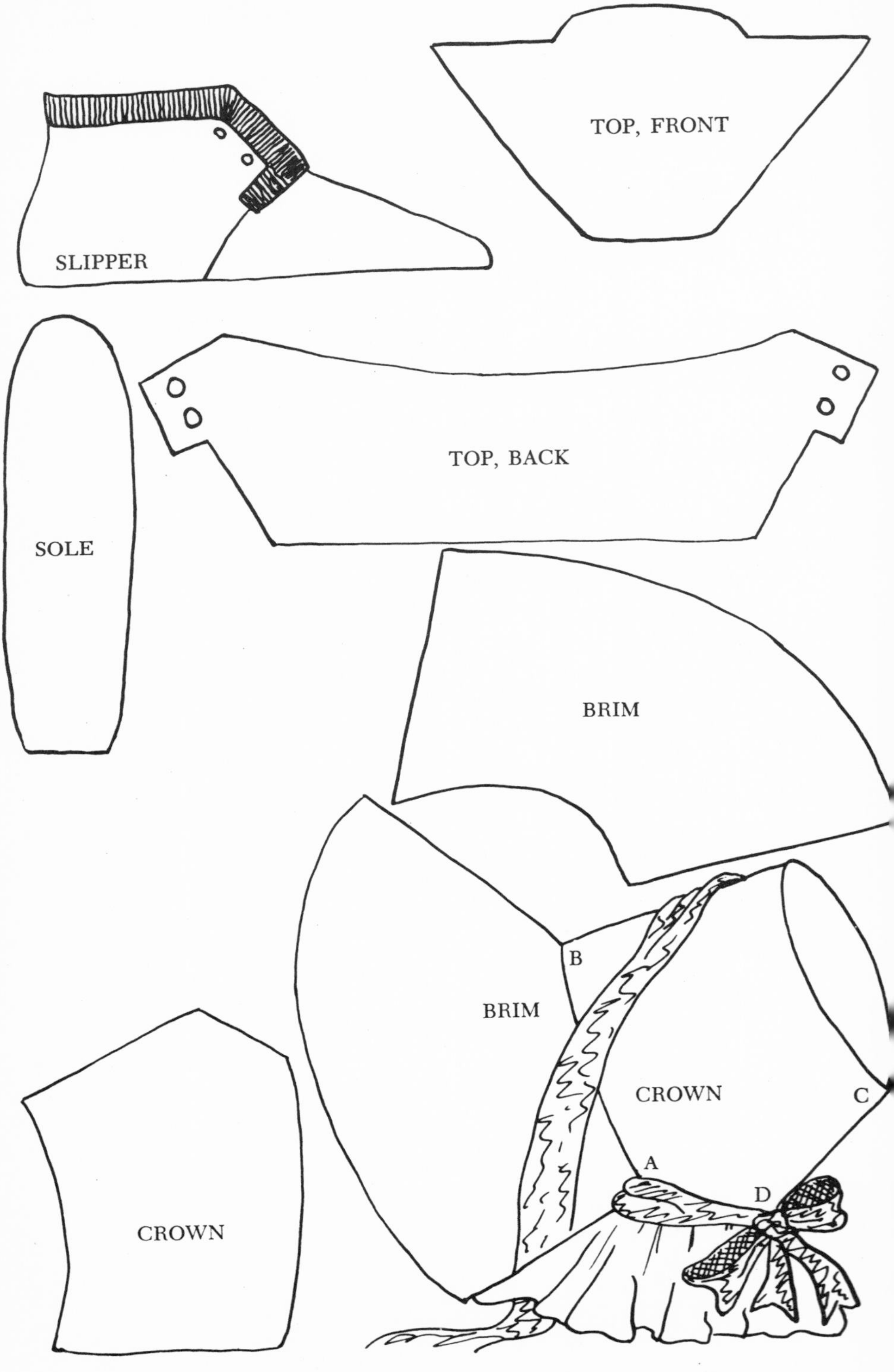

SLIPPER

TOP, FRONT

TOP, BACK

SOLE

BRIM

BRIM

B

CROWN

A

C

D

CROWN

The bottom of the bodice was pointed, skirt quite full and without trimming.

With the pink gown, the doll wore a pair of bronze leather French boots, bound with brown grosgrain. Notice the shape of the sole. Ribbon laces go through the eyelets. The brown grosgrain binding is sewn on last.

Quite characteristic of the period is the wax doll's pink satin bonnet. The crown and brim are cut as shown. In order to achieve the perfection and professional quality of the Paris original, it will be necessary to cut two pieces for the brim (facing and top) and a matching but trifle smaller piece of crinoline with which to stiffen it. Stitch outside edges of brim together, turn inside out and press carefully. Slip in crinoline piece. The crown also needs the stiffening of crinoline. Crown is joined along line C-D and is joined to brim along A-B. The straight line, D-A, goes across the back of the neck. A soft bias fold of material is gathered into back of bonnet and sewn to bottom sides of brim. Trim as shown.

FASHIONS OF THE 1860's

The patterns on the following page should first be cut in tissue and fitted to the doll. Sizes and shapes vary so that no specific measurements can be given, for each doll is an individual problem. Once having perfected a master pattern, any number of minor changes may be made to give variety to the styling.

1. This bodice was originally designed in 1860 as the top of a petticoat. By making long sleeves and a high neck it becomes the type of basque characteristic of the covered wagon period. By lengthening the back peplum and bringing it down to a long oval, the bodice becomes an outer jacket with long sleeves, of course. As it is, it is a charming little bodice for a summer frock.

2. Sheer cotton chemise worn under the corset and drawers.

3. Hoopskirt. Make like a full petticoat but allow enough depth for tucks wide enough to hold the hoops. These may be made of thin rattan canes (balloon sticks). Top cane should be shortest, bottom the longest.

1

2

3

4

5A

5B

5C

5D

4. Ball gown using basic bodice 1, hoopskirt 3 and overskirt of your own designing. The embroidered flounces and bow trim are typical.

5. Cut a flat oval and slash at solid lines (A, top). Dotted line indicates shape of top. Lap the slashes to get crown. Tack down. Cut a larger oval (B), make slashes top and bottom; cut out center. Fold back along dotted line to make brim. Sew crown into brim (C). Trim (D) with ostrich tips, ribbon bows and ribbon streamers.

CHRISTMAS DAY AT THE ORPHANAGE

This charming group is made up with the same fidelity to details that marks the other
Christmas windows assembled and staged by James McCreery. The dolls in this and the
other windows were from Mrs. Sidney Howell's collection. The Museum of the City of
New York loaned the doll's furniture and other accessories. The babies in the canopied
bed are 20th century Bye-Lo babies designed by Gladys Storey Putnam; the nurse and her
two small charges are 19th century bisque. The bed is made of two footstools pushed
together. Its dust ruffle matches the canopy and curtains and could be easily duplicated to
make an unusually effective set for one or two of your own baby dolls.

10.

Fitting Backgrounds for Dolls

DOLLS MUST LIVE SOMEWHERE. WE FIND THE IMPULSE
to give them a background all their own almost irresistible after
we have once seen the dolls in a setting of furniture scaled to their
proportions. It may be only a small display furnished with a few
articles chosen to accent the realistic quality of the dolls or it may
be an extremely elaborate dolls' house complete in every tiny
detail.

A DRAMATIC DISPLAY AT CHRISTMAS TIME

The possibilities inherent in a single display designed to dramatize a group of dolls was most enchantingly demonstrated by the
series of Christmas windows created by James McCreery & Co.,
New York City, a few years ago. This New York department store
devoted all its Christmas windows to doll groupings which
included antique doll furniture and decorative accessories.

An exceptionally fine china shoulder-head doll stands beside an equally fine miniature maple highboy that probably was a cabinetmaker's sample. Nineteenth century toys and child-sized chairs combine quite happily even if they are not in scale with each other. The overall effect has liveliness and charm that, interesting as the doll is, would be lacking if she stood there in an empty background. The scene above is part of the Vaughan Collection.

A serpentine-fronted mahogany chest (another cabinetmaker's sample), baby sleds and 19th century toys make up another group in which a rare leather-head doll sits. These displays and the large view of the Vaughan Collection on the following page bear study for they dramatically illustrate the effectiveness of making a stage set to show off your dolls. The alert doll shop proprietor should collect such props (not necessarily antiques).

The dolls in this Vaughan Collection grouping vary considerably in both size and type of materials, china, bisque, composition, wood and rag being represented. The furniture, some crudely made while other pieces are fine, provides a lived-in look that heightens interest in the dolls themselves.

By giving each one a theme, such as "Christmas Day at the Orphanage," the store assembled the varied groups and styles of dolls in the dramatic window settings. It took imagination and ingenuity of a high order to arrange more than fifty groups of dolls and their furniture so delightfully that passers-by and window-shoppers stopped to enjoy their artful appeal and spent hours examining them.

Small Group Can Be Effective. Skilled professionals were responsible for the assembling of the material and the set up of the displays. The results are worthy of study and adaptation by the doll collector who may, unconsciously, be a bit weary of seeing a perfectly static line up of dolls, lovely as they may be. It is not necessary to have a warehouse full of doll furniture and accessories. A few pieces, rearranged frequently, will be a source of continual interest. One does not even need a special custom-built background. A three-fold screen made of corrugated board or plywood, about three feet high, and covered with gay wallpaper, will be a most effective background. Treated as the walls of a room, with miniature pictures hanging on them, one or two pieces of doll-size furniture and two or three dolls—and there you have a display!

Another part of the Vaughan Collection sets off a group of small wooden dolls. In the foreground the tea table is set with miniature pewter. The chairs and tables and the miniature linen press in the lower right corner are all fine examples of child-sized furniture while the pieces near the wooden dolls were made expressly for dolls.

In arranging the dolls, have a definite idea in mind of what the dolls are supposed to be doing: "A Sewing Party," "Afternoon Tea," "Breaking the News to Mother," "Packing for the Journey," "Between the Dark and the Daylight,"—any theme which will give a reason for posing the dolls in a particular position. Such themes also stimulate the imagination in the selection of the various accessories which may be included in the display.

A FAMOUS COLLECTION IN A TINY CHURCH

The Vaughan Doll Collection at the Essex Institute in Salem, Mass., is a comprehensive assortment of 19th century dolls, miniature furniture, toys and accessories. Housed in a tiny church which had been moved to the grounds of the Institute for this express purpose, this collection is most interesting, as it so clearly demonstrates the value of adroit arrangement. It matters little that many of the pieces of furniture and the dolls are out of scale with each other. To some extent this but adds attractiveness to the entire display. The photographs of the Vaughan Collection, shown here, illustrate the various groups to even better advantage than if you were to see them in person, for the plate glass which shields the collection produces an annoying glare and reflection on the whole display.

Doll furniture made by author can be used as a single room setting to display dolls in or for furnishing a scale model doll house. The chair really rocks and the leaves of the Pembroke table actually open up. The picture on the wall was cut from a magazine and framed. Furniture was scaled to go with the mother-daughter dolls below, mother being a 9½ inch Penny Wooden type carved and dressed by the author; daughter is Samantha, shown on page 125, also made by the author. A little stage setting like this always helps the display.

11.

Making a Doll House

SOONER OR LATER, THE ENTHUSIASTIC DOLL MAKER IS GO-
ing to be faced with the urge to make a doll house. This may be
prompted by the young daughter or granddaughter insisting that
life is not worth living until she has one. Or it may simply grow
because the idea itself is a tantalizing and intriguing one. What-
ever the motive, the building of a doll house is a fascinating com-
plement to the making of dolls. Once the house is completed, it
offers an invitation to make dolls to take up residence there.

There is a good deal of work attached to building a doll house.
You might just as well make a good one as a poor one. The labor
involved is about equal in both instances. But what a difference!

"SCALE" FOR THE HOUSE

A good doll house is one that, like good dolls, is in perfect
scale. The accomplishment of perfect scale is not difficult. It only
needs preliminary planning. If you intend to furnish the doll
house with chairs, etc., from the five and ten cent stores—and

243

they do have an extremely wide assortment of doll furniture—buy a few pieces before you start the house. Keep these pieces before you as you work to guide the placement of ceilings, and the sizes of doors and windows. This type of doll furniture is not built "to scale," as they say in the field of art, architecture and the making of miniatures. These ten-cent-store pieces are smaller than are "scale" pieces which are designed according to the rule of 1 inch to the foot.

USING CARTONS

Very satisfactory doll houses may be made of corrugated cartons from the grocery store. They come in various sizes. If you tell the manager what you want them for he will pick out those in good condition. Get an assortment of sizes and experiment with them. Set a large one and a small one side by side. Turn the large one on end so that the smaller one looks like a wing. Now the outside shape is beginning to take form. How many rooms will it contain? Set a couple of the plastic furniture pieces in the bottom of one carton. Hold a piece of paper over them, moving it up or down until it is about two and one-half times as high as a chair. That gives you the position of the ceiling. Mark the position on the inner side of the carton. Is there room for three floors or only two with a small space above the upper one? Remember, three floors require more furniture and accessories. Perhaps you'd better try a smaller carton.

When you have decided upon the size of the cartons to be used, take them back to the super-market and ask the manager to staple them together. He has a special stapler for these boxes and it will take him just about half a minute to do this for you. It makes a very strong join.

If the combination of a large and a smaller carton is used, similar to the sketch shown here, let the taller one become two rooms and let the wing provide space for a combination kitchen and dining room. This produces a three-room house which is ample for this initial venture into house building.

Cutting Windows and Doors. The front of this type of doll house is left open. Have some idea of the furniture to be used before cutting windows and doors. Actually no door is necessary in this house, although one might be cut through from the living room to the dining-kitchen. Windows should be placed about 2 inches from the floor and end about ½ to ¼ inch below the ceiling. A good standard width for the windows is about 3 inches. Rule them carefully and cut them out with a razor blade or mat knife. Keep the edges as straight and clean as possible. Now paint the entire outside of the house, using one of the water-mixed wall paints.

The window trim for the outside may be fashioned from ⅜-inch strips of white paper pasted neatly around each window. Shutters are easily made from the pieces cut from the window. Cut each piece in half from top to bottom. Paint the pieces dark green or red or black. With a soft lead pencil draw on the lines indicating the louvers or crosspieces of the shutter. Use a white crayon pencil on black paint. The shutters are attached by means of Scotch tape.

Wallpaper from Gift Wrappings. The inside of the house may be painted or papered. The latter covers imperfections more effectively and adds a gay and authentic note, providing you can find paper having a design small enough to look right. Look at gift wrapping papers. Many of them are printed with small colorful designs that are just right for this purpose. Measure the inside walls carefully and paste on the paper smoothly, using a wad of absorbent cotton to work out wrinkles. Let the wallpaper cover the window openings. It can be cut out later with the mat knife used from the outside of the house.

The ceiling of the living room forms the floor of the bedroom. Take pains to measure this accurately, allowing ½ inch at either side to be bent up. Cement is spread evenly along the bent up portions which are then placed against the side walls of the house. See that the ceiling is in straight and does not sag at the back. Ease it into position and hold it with the hands for a moment or two until the cement takes hold. The bent up part acts as a base board in the bedroom. Cut another strip to match and cement it along the back wall.

CLOSE-UP OF
UPSTAIRS
FLOORING
AND WINDOW
DETAILS

LIVING ROOM
WINDOW AND
WALL
DECORATION

Putting in Floors. Now paint or paper the living room. The floor should have an extra piece cemented on to make a firm and even surface. Thin plywood or prestwood, cut to size, makes excellent flooring and gives weight to the bottom of the house. After the walls and floor have been finished, add baseboards similar to those in the bedroom.

The kitchen decorating is done in the same way. It, too, requires an extra floor. This room might be very attractive if done in small checked gingham or a tiny bright plaid cotton which can be pasted on just like paper. After the walls are done, the inside frame of all windows are finished. This is most easily done with ¼-inch strips of colored Scotch tape pasted around each window.

A GABLE ROOF

As it is, the house has a flat roof which is not too attractive. A V-shape or gable roof is easy to construct with colored poster board. Measure the width of the house and add 1 inch to each side. Measure the depth of the house and add 4 inches to that measurement. This gives the outside measurement of the rectangle which will make the roof. The card is bent in half along the width and then set on top of the house. The open ends are filled in with triangles cut to fit. The roof is attached to the triangles on the inside with book binding linen tape which is gummed on one side. Set the roof on the house and, with the same gummed tape, attach it to the house under the eaves. Follow the same procedure for roof of wing, only make the pitch of the roof less sharp. In measuring for the wing roof, allow but one extra inch on the width, as the other side of the roof fits flush to the house.

All that remains to be done now is to furnish the house. Having started with plastic furniture from the dime stores, and having gauged the ceiling heights accordingly, the rest of the house must be furnished with the same style things. The introduction of larger size pieces, no matter how attractive they may be, will throw the perfection of the whole house out of kilter. Be consistent and avoid using any pieces or accessories which are out of scale to this particular house. Curtains, draperies, bed clothing, cushions, rugs,

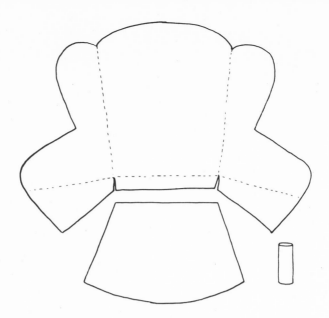

Actual size pattern for an upholstered arm chair. Cut shape from heavy poster board, score along dotted lines, bending arm pieces forward and bottom flanges up. Paste in place, then paste in seat. Legs are short pieces of ¼-inch dowels. Upholster inside of chair with cotton batting and cover with fabric, adding ruffle bottom to conceal legs.

you will make, cutting them to careful measure and pressing each thing before it is installed. The finished house will have a definite charm that will whet your appetite to make another.

A REAL SCALE THIS TIME

Let this second doll house be truly a scale one, in that it will conform to the rule of 1 inch to the foot. Again, cartons may be used but this time select somewhat larger ones. Since ceiling heights must be not more than 9 inches for the living room and 7½ to 8 inches for the bedrooms and kitchen, you will want cartons that give you generous width as well as usable height. The decoration of the house follows the same general lines as the first house. The furniture used in this house is scaled 1 inch to the foot, as are all the accessories to be used.

The main differences, aside from that of scale, between this house and the first one is that you will want to make many of the pieces of furniture used in it. Yes, you can buy real miniature pieces of beautiful workmanship and perfect scaling. But they are

DOLL BED WITH LACE TRIMMED CANOPY

not cheap. Several bought pieces will add realness and charm to
the finished house, although the majority of pieces will have been
the product of your own hands. What is most alluring about a
house of this scale is the great variety of inexpensive decorating
accessories that may be purchased for it at relatively small cost.
The plastic pots and pans of the dime store fit this house better
than they would the first house. Miniature glass jugs, pitchers,
vases, perfectly scaled, are frequently found in dime, novelty, and
department stores. The jugs and vases may be turned into delightful little lamps, or used to hold wee sprays of flowers in them.

Miniature Furnishings. If expense is not too important, sterling
silver miniatures may be bought at not too high prices. Only a
very few pieces are necessary to give a rich and distinguished note.
Patient search will find all manner of miniature fruit and food
replicas as well as knives, forks and spoons. Birthday candles
shortened and scraped down will grace tiny candelabra that are
sometimes found in the larger dime stores. Look, too, for miniature
reproductions in brass of fireplace equipment.

This is not a house to be rushed through, but progressed with
and enjoyed over a good period of time. The cartons, when stapled
together and further reinforced with gummed tape along the
joinings, are remarkably sturdy, a factor which is increased by the

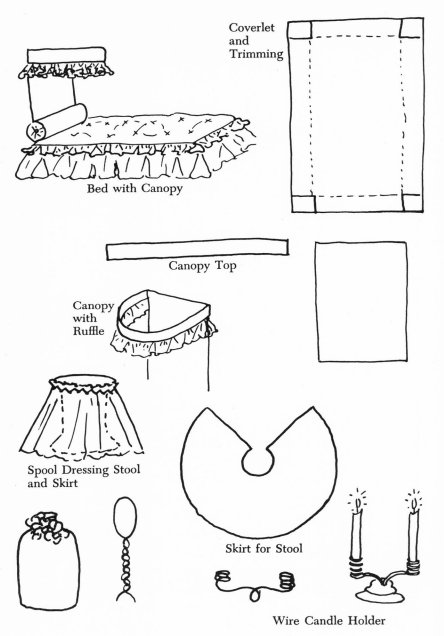

Coverlet
and
Trimming

Bed with Canopy

Canopy Top

Canopy
with
Ruffle

Spool Dressing Stool
and Skirt

Skirt for Stool

Wire Candle Holder

DRAWINGS OF BEDROOM FURNISHINGS

Left:
Bureau with
Mirror and
Spool Stands

Below:
Wire
Chair

DRAWINGS OF BUREAU AND CHAIR

painting and inner papering. Consequently, it is not wasteful of time, effort and some money to expend them on a "paper" house.

HOW TO MAKE FURNITURE

Several patterns for homemade furniture and accessories are given on these pages. With them you can achieve a truly handsome group of pieces. They are easy to follow and are as easily changed and adapted to suit your specific needs. The upholstered chair with its engaging flounce fits as well into the bedroom as it does in the living room. Only the choice of fabric used to cover it determines its setting. Straight chairs are equally versatile, being appropriate for any room in the house.

Pedestal tables are simply made from wooden spools with tops cut from heavy cardboard or poster board, or thin plywood. Paint or stain completes them. Investigate your children's toy box for likely sized wooden blocks, especially unfinished maple ones. They have an infinite variety of uses which will immediately become apparent as you try setting them around the doll house rooms. Long narrow ones may become window seats. Short narrow ones, set on end, make good lamp tables. Tiny square ones may have a padded top and a floor length ruffle pasted on to form attractive hassocks or dressing table stools.

MINIATURE ORNAMENTS FOR DECORATIONS

A FAMILY OF DOLLS

Once the house is completed—which it need never be, for it is simple to add on a wing to take care of those miniature treasures you have been picking up—dolls to go with the house are the next step. Once again, the question of scale enters the picture. Father doll should be 6 inches tall, while mother is 5 inches. Children are scaled accordingly. These dolls are best made of pipe stem cleaners, having feet of self-hardening clay which will enable them to stand unsupported. A ball of self-hardening clay molded about the size of a small robin's egg may be used for the head. This is done right around the head loop of the wire and allowed to harden on it. Features are painted on when head is dry. Clothes, because of their minute size, must be of the simplest. Father's clothes are the most difficult. Use dark cottons or rayons, not wool. Lap the seams and hold them together with cement. Select a fabric which does not fray easily so that you can avoid the necessity of hems. When the doll house family moves in they will fit so beautifully into their delightful surroundings that you will find it difficult to remember the many hours required to produce this charming and perfect miniature.

12.

Doll Language and Definitions

SHOP TALK IS ALWAYS FASCINATING FOR THOSE WHO ARE familiar with it. It is equally confusing to the uninitiated. When it comes to dolls it is necessary to master a certain amount of doll terminology. This enables you to appreciate various examples when you are handling them and also serves as a guide in determining the real value of the dolls.

In the broad classifications of wood, wax, china, etc., given in an earlier chapter, there are certain words and terms that qualify individual examples of each. Sometimes these qualifying terms are proper names, trademark letters or symbols, initials, numbers or national names. At other times the qualifying terms are purely descriptive and accepted generally to indicate specific types. Instead of spreading these names, terms and phrases throughout the book, we give them here in a group. The terms include types of dolls from many lands and cover a comprehensive period of history. They are terms which are everyday language to collectors and dealers.

WOOD

PENNY WOODENS: *Early 18th to 20th century*
Hand carved in pine, poplar or maple by German and Tyrolean toymakers. Later they were made in New England. They have hourglass figures, slender necks, sloping shoulders. Legs and arms are jointed at shoulders, elbows, hips and knees. In the small sizes, the lower arms terminate in points with no indication of hands. Heads vary in shape. Some are quite round, others are slightly pointed on top. Hair is painted black and always indicates a center part at forehead. The actual Penny Wooden sold for a penny in New England about the middle of the 19th century. She was under 4 inches in height. Larger sizes which are higher priced are almost identical, but have more elaborate hair-dos, with some attempt at carved hands and features. The hair-dos are sometimes achieved by means of composition added and molded to the head. These wood dolls vary in size from ¾ inch to about 12 inches.

PEGGITY DOLLS: *1935*
These are modern adaptations of the Penny Woodens. They are made in Rhode Island by Marion I. Perkins and come in doll-house size.

QUEEN ANNE: *1664–1714*
There are two types of the Queen Anne dòll extant. One is entirely of wood with bamboo hands having ugly, fork-like fingers. The other and more attractive type is also of wood but has had the face and shoulders covered with a thin plaster coating. This one usually has hands that are carved more delicately and realistically. Inset glass eyes and wigs of human hair are characteristic. Genuine Queen Annes were beautifully dressed. Fine linen, real lace, lovely brocades and exquisite quilting were used to duplicate the fashions of the time.

PEG DOLLS:
So called because they are jointed by means of wooden pegs that allow the limbs to move easily, as in the Penny Woodens. "Peg" is also used to denote the shape of a primi-

The one-piece molded doll with stationary arms and legs became known as a "Frozen Charlotte," a name derived from an old ballad of the 1860's. They came in a wide variety of materials and had as wide a variety of hair-dos. This elaborately gowned Frozen Charlotte has a more delicately modeled face than many of them. She is about 6 inches high and is of a fine quality of china.

WITCH AND WIZARD DOLLS

Modern stump dolls (a single piece of wood instead of legs) made in India in 1938 for the tourist trade. Exotically costumed as Hindu dancers, their heads, arms and upper bodies are of cloth. The features are embroidered.

tively carved wooden head and torso. The word "carved" is almost a misnomer as the characteristic appearance of the Peg head is that of a crudely turned but otherwise flat piece of wood. Features were painted on.

STUMP DOLL: *Late 17th–18th century*
This type has the same crudely turned, flattish head with the neck indicated slightly and some curving done for the shoulders and breast. In back, below the neck and to the bottom of the so-called torso, the wood is perfectly flat looking as if it had been sliced off. The stump doll was frequently without legs of any sort. Its arms were held on by means of the dress or underwear. Arms were of cloth or of wood.

This bald baby has a composition head and inset glass eyes. The arms and legs are also of composition and articulated by means of cloth joinings. The head can be made to nod by means of a rod that is worked from beneath its long dress.

BLOCKHEAD:
Another term for the Stump doll.

FLANDERS' BABIES: *Early 19th century*
These are very similar to the Penny Woodens but were made in the Netherlands. They were exported to England in quantity and were the kind of doll used by Queen Victoria for her childhood collection. A popular jingle current during their hey-day ran:

*"The children of England take pleasure in breaking
What the children of Flanders take pleasure in making."*

LAY FIGURE: *Middle Ages—20th century*
Actually not a doll but an artist's wooden model or mannequin. It is ball-jointed throughout: elbows, shoulders, wrists,

hips, knees, ankles, waist and throat. The features are finely delineated as are the hands and feet. It is interesting to compare it with the ball-jointed wooden doll that appeared in the 19th century. The lay figure or mannequin was first designed in Italy during the late Middle Ages for the use of artists and sculptors. It was brought to this country where it is supposed to have served as a model for skillful whittlers who carved facsimiles of it, then turned the facsimiles into dolls by adding wigs. There is, of course, no proof that the original mannequin was not so adorned to transform it into a doll. It is claimed that several of these mannequins date from the early and mid-18th century. Since a comparatively modern one can *look* very old, it would take an expert in woods to verify the supposed antiquity of the early lay figure. So far, no wood expert has made any statement concerning them. Lay figures may be purchased today in any artists' supply store. Wood ones are no different in detail and workmanship from the lay figures of the 18th century.

JOEL ELLIS: 1873

Except for the hands and feet which were of iron, the Joel Ellis doll was of wood. The Ellis doll patent covered his particular type of mortise and tenon friction joints which allowed the dolls to be put into all sorts of dancing and acrobatic positions. The heads, pressed into form under hydraulic pressure, were of rock maple. They were stationary. Heads, shoulders, arms and legs were painted. The shoes of Ellis dolls are always black. All Ellis dolls have curled fingers. The dolls were made in three sizes, 12, 15 and 18 inches. Some Negro dolls were made from the same head mold but had the Negro color painted on. These dolls were manufactured only during 1873, consequently there are not too many of them to be found.

MASON AND TAYLOR: 1879–1882

An improvement, insofar as the joints were concerned, over the Ellis doll. It had a combination ball and socket with the mortise and tenon. Feet were of lead or pewter. Early dolls had wooden hands, later ones matched the feet. Fingers were always extended in a straight pose. The bodies, arms and legs, and core of the head were of wood. The outer coating of the head, used to model the features, was of composition.

WITCH AND WIZARD DOLLS: *About 1880*

Made by Mason and Taylor, they did not have the patented features of the regular M. & T. dolls. Their legs and arms were shapely and jointed only at the hips with wood pins and at shoulders with steel pins. The shoes were painted blue and had oriental turned up toes. A curious feature is the toggle joint which attached the head to the body. By means of this contrivance the head can apparently be cut off from the neck, yet it remains on the doll. They were dressed in loose garments of bright cottons, resembling kimonos in style. These dolls were made for export to Japan, the country where decapitation was the ordinary method of capital punishment.

JOHNSON HEAD: *Patented, 1882*

A patented head, used by Mason and Taylor, consisting of a composition over a wood core.

SANDERS JOINT: *Patented, 1880*

An improvement on the ball and socket mortised joints. Used in Mason and Taylor dolls.

MARTIN DOLL: *1879*

Obviously made on the same machines which turned out the Mason and Taylor dolls, this wood doll is distinguished by a spiral spring or elastic which passes through the upper torso from shoulder to shoulder. In every other respect the doll is identical with the earlier Mason and Taylor dolls. Not many were made.

SPRINGFIELD DOLLS: *1872–1882*

Wood dolls made in Springfield, Vt., by Joel Ellis, Martin, and Mason and Taylor. It is believed that the so-called Martin doll was actually an early Mason and Taylor (see above). The Sanders joints and the Johnson heads were used in the Mason and Taylor dolls. In 1881, a patent was granted to Mason and Taylor for their first movable head. Prior to that date all of their heads were stationary.

SCHOENHUT DOLL: *1909–1924*

An all-wood doll fully articulated (wrists and ankles as well as knees, hips, elbows, shoulders) by means of steel springs and swivel joints. Practically indestructible, they were painted with durable oil enamels. The models for the heads were life-like and fairly attractive. Hair was either carved or of wigs. Eyes were either painted or of glass set in, either fixed or movable. Every Schoenhut doll had two holes in the bottom of each foot so that the doll might be stood in any desired position on the stand which came with it. Later (1924) Schoenhut dolls were jointed with elastic cord while some styles had stuffed bodies and mamma voices, but retained the wooden heads. These dolls were made in infants, young babies and little boy and girl styles. The rarest of the Schoenhut dolls is the mannequin designed for artists and window display pieces. Only a thousand of them were manufactured. They appeared in 1915. While some of them were sold, many of them were junked when the business closed down in 1924.

PEDLAR DOLL: *Mid-18th to mid-19th century*

The older, original Pedlar dolls were of wood similar in style to the Penny Woodens. The distinguishing features of their costumes were the red capes and black hoods worn over white mob caps. Gowns and aprons varied. Suspended around the necks were flat trays or baskets upon which was an amazing and absorbing collection, in miniature, of the items usually sold by their human prototypes, the Notion Nannies of Old England. Authentic Pedlar dolls are extremely rare. Sometimes, the heads and faces are of composition over the original wood. Some Pedlar dolls of wax or china have been found, while much later, "assembled" Pedlar dolls have appeared. These latter ones are fairly modern, costumed to resemble the older dolls and having trays or baskets of wares assembled to complete the outfit.

SPOON HANDS:

A semi-carved wood hand with thumb indicated. In appearance not unlike a wooden mixing spoon. Used by home whittlers as well as by Mason and Taylor and found on some of the larger Penny Woodens.

A late 19th century wooden doll from Germany has arms that are articulated by means of cloth tops tacked to shoulders. It is probable that the arms and legs are replacements. The well-defined nose and style of the painted eyes dates her no earlier than the mid-1880's. She is 11 inches tall.

This finely costumed blonde bisque doll and baby may be of French manufacture. She dates from the 1880's and has a professionally made cloth body and
legs and feet. The costume is pretty rather than authentic. It is unusual to find
an original pair in such perfect condition.

CHINA

There are three grades of china: blue white, creamy white and flesh-toned, the latter being known as pink luster. China heads are modeled in clay, glazed and then fired at a high temperature in a kiln. The all-over coloring and the evenness of its tone is indicative of the grade of the finished article: blue white being most common, the creamy being better and the so-called pink luster the best. It is understood that, although we call them dolls, we are actually discussing and defining doll heads. Contrary to other material classifications (wood, rag, etc.), so-called china dolls had bodies made of cloth or kid. Arms and legs may be of matching china or may be of the body material. There is only one all-china doll. It is called a Frozen Charlotte and is defined below.

Prior to 1891, all merchandise came into this country with no indication of its place of origin. After that date, all imported merchandise had to be marked with the name of the country in which it was made. That is why the majority of china doll heads found here bear no identifying marks or names. However, some china dolls, purchased after 1891 in countries other than the United States, and brought back as gifts, are not marked with the country of origin. A careful analysis of details and styling should be made before dating that kind of doll earlier than 1890. There are, however, a number of generally accepted terms and phrases used to identify china heads.

SHOULDER-HEAD:

Head, neck, shoulders and bosom in one piece.

DEEP SHOULDER:

The older china head was modeled so that the sloping shoulders were deep enough to allow for the low-cut, off-shoulder fashions that were popular during the first half of the nineteenth century. As fashions changed, and the low-cut gown became more of an evening dress than a daytime gown, the shoulders of the china head were shortened.

SWIVEL-NECKED:

There were some china heads made which allowed the head to be turned from side to side. This device, however, more common in bisque, is very rare in china.

Countess Dagmar head with center part and tightly curled coiffure pulled up into horn-like peaks on the sides.

Germanic type of china head, showing knob-like black curls. The face is broad cheeked and heavy jowled.

Empress Eugenie head with tresses brushed softly back from the face, and bands of ribbon holding curls low on the neck.

DOLL HEADS OF THE NINETEENTH CENTURY

OVAL EYE:

The painted eyes of the older china heads were definitely oval; i. e., they were long in shape as compared with the obviously round-eyed style that appeared later on.

SQUAT NECK:

A very short, rather thick neck characteristic of the late 19th to early 20th century china heads. A short neck, not necessarily a thick one, was used to denote a *child* doll as contrasted with a *lady* doll whose neck was definitely longer and more slender. During the period when children's hair styles duplicated those of their elders, the shorter neck was the only means of denoting an age difference.

FANCIES:

Any china shoulder-head in which extra details were added such as contrasting colored hair ribbons, snoods, bands,

Mary Todd Lincoln head, front and back view, with net snood and side rosette trimming.

Adelina Patti head, showing smooth top hair-do parted in center and dressed behind ears with low clusters of ringlets.

Jenny Lind head with black hair parted in the middle and smoothed back into long low-hanging tiers of curls.

DOLL HEADS OF THE NINETEENTH CENTURY

combs, guimpes, earrings (or the pierced holes for them), and necklaces.

BALL HEAD:

A china shoulder-head devoid of modeled or painted hair, usually having a black cloth circle on crown of head to which a wig may be pasted.

BIEDERMEIER:

Another name for Ball head (see above). This name is taken from a period of furniture making and decoration originating in Germany. The Biedermeier period is conceded to have covered the years 1816–1848, but the period of 1820–1830 represents the best. When found with the original body and china legs, the Biedermeier doll shows the flat, heelless shoe worn from the very late 18th century through the 1840's.

FROZEN CHARLOTTE:

This is a one-piece molded doll with no joints or other form of articulation. It was made in other materials as well as china and ranged in size from one to twelve inches. Usually definitely chubby in shape, it came in a wide variety of grades and decoration. Many of them, despite their nudity, wore ruffled and ribboned bonnets. Others had contrasting hair ribbons. Hair styles and colors were as numerous as one could desire. The feet were separated, the upper legs, usually, joined together above the knee. Hands were always extended and the fingers held close together, slightly curled and pointing down. The old name for this type is "Pillar." The popular name, "Frozen Charlotte," seems to have been derived from an old ballad of the 1860's which told the sad tale of Fair Charlotte, so eager to go sparking with her beau on a Vermont winter night that she wore only a silken cloak. Yes, she froze, literally.

JENNY LIND:

Supposedly a portrait head of the famous Swedish singer who was so popular here during her concert tours from 1850–52. She was brought to this country by P. T. Barnum, the great showman, who billed her as the "Swedish Nightingale." The resemblance of the china doll head to the singer was more in the hair-do than in the facial features. Actually, Jenny Lind was a blonde but preferred dark hair, so she always wore a dark wig on the concert stage. All Jenny Lind china doll heads have dark hair. Since molds were used for a considerable length of time, the Jenny Lind mold was probably used for many years after the singer had retired about 1853. Therefore, it is stretching a point in the question of dating to place all Jenny Lind china doll heads in the early 1850's.

COUNTESS DAGMAR:

Supposedly a portrait head of Countess Dagmar, mother of Nicholas II, last Czar of Russia, its identifying feature is the hair-do. The china heads always have black hair with several short curls at the center of the forehead. The hair is curled back, away from the face, and is finished in back with two horizontal puffs at the nape of the neck. A band or comb tops off the upper puff. Also considered a "Dagmar" is a similar hair style which has but one puff. The Countess Dagmar comes also in Parian but with blonde hair.

MARY TODD LINCOLN:

Wife of Abraham Lincoln, this lady was characterized by a plump face, small and rather pinched features, and an obviously double chin. The fancied resemblance of some dolls to Mrs. Lincoln has resulted in a whole group of china heads being so named. As practically every china head in this country originated in Germany, and because Mrs. Lincoln's fame was definitely local rather than international (Jenny Lind, Queen Victoria, etc.), it is extremely doubtful that any German manufacturer of china doll heads made a "portrait" head of Mary Todd Lincoln. The hair styles of doll heads in this group vary, although all have center parts with the hair lifted away from the temples. About 1860–1866.

ALICE IN WONDERLAND:

Definitely a child's head, the hair is brushed back from the forehead, held by a band which circles the top of the head and ends at the ears. The hair falls straight to the nape of the neck. Named for the little girl in *Alice in Wonderland* by Lewis Carroll, which was published in 1865, the doll head is very similar to the illustration of Alice by Sir John Tenniel.

ADELINA PATTI:

Another famous singer who made her New York debut in 1859. Prior to that date, and long after, she was internationally famous. Heads that are claimed to resemble the singer have the conventional center hair part, with vertical curls starting at the ears and clustered around the lower back of the head. The resemblance is fictitious.

EUGENIE:

Wife of Napoleon III, Empress Eugenie reigned in Paris from 1853 to 1870. A very beautiful woman, she exerted great influence in the field of fashion. The doll head named for her was quite probably a portrait of her. The features are finer and have more character than was usual. The hair-do, having six or seven longish curls falling from beneath double puffs at the back of the head, closely approximated Eugenie's own style of coiffure.

DOTTER DOLL:
This name refers to a doll patented in 1880 by Charles T. Dotter, of Brooklyn, N. Y. While the patent referred to the cloth body which had corsets printed on the fabric, the Dotter doll heads were of china imported from Germany. The Dotter heads are one of the few china heads having a patent mark on the china. On the lower part of the back of the shoulder-piece is the legend "Patented Dec. 7/80."

GOLDSMITH DOLL:
Another American doll whose patent covered the body rather than the head. This, too, was a corset doll, patented in 1885. The china heads were imported from Germany.

QUEEN VICTORIA:
Straight hair parted in center, having the front sections braided and looped down and around the ears, exposing rather than hiding them, to join a bun at back of head. The features of the face were not too dissimilar from those of the young queen. This type dated in the early 1840's.

BRUSH MARKS:
Many of the finer china heads had delicately painted fine lines joining the hair-do to the face to simulate the natural hair line. The majority of the heads made no attempt to soften the hair line; the face stopped and the hair started in a harsh and definite way.

MONA LISA:
Face longer and more slender than in usual run of china heads. Hair, center parted, straight to tops of ears, then clustered curls. The smile is cryptic and rather mysterious, as is characteristic of the painting "Mona Lisa" by Leonardo da Vinci. Some collectors have called this type "Florence Nightingale."

DOLLY MADISON:
Another double-chinned doll head. Sausage curls and center part, this time indicated by a white line, are the characteristic points of the head. Facial features are better proportioned and not so close together as is true of the Mary Todd Lincoln dolls.

Many other names of famous women crop up in the descriptions of doll heads. For the most part, they are fanciful terms with no basis of fact. Many of them have grown up through "sales talk," a natural if somewhat careless way of intriguing a customer's interest. The variety of expressions, hair-dos, and skin colorings offer wide scope to the imaginative person. By stretching the imagination, it is quite possible to see a "resemblance" to practically any famous woman. On the other hand, collectors, as well as the average owner, have a propensity for naming their dolls. Sometimes these names are those of actual women, either past or present, more usually they are old-fashioned names selected because of their appropriateness to the character of the doll. The names have nothing to do with the dating or typing of the dolls in question.

BISQUE

The main difference between china and bisque is easily recognized; china has a high glaze while bisque has a dull, soft-looking surface. The color of china heads is controlled by the basic color of the clay and the tone of the glaze which is applied before firing. The flesh color of bisque is controlled by the artistry and color sense of the manufacturer since it is an artificial color also applied to the clay before firing. This color, really a glaze, sinks into the porous surface of the clay and is fused therein, making it permanent. This can be seen by examining the edges of a broken bisque piece. The color has actually penetrated some little distance into the surface of the clay. The so-called "French Bisque" has a faint flesh color ground into the clay before modeling and firing. This is the finest bisque of all.

As early as 1844, bisque heads were being used on dolls that

TWO BEAUTIFUL
BISQUE
DOLL HEADS

The sweet-faced girl doll,
her ears pierced for ear-
rings, according to the
vogue on the Continent
when she was made.
Her eyes are brown. The
baby doll has blue eyes
and a fine modeled face.

were manufactured in France. While the majority of bisque heads came, as usual, from Germany, smaller quantities came from France and, much later on, from Japan. During World War I, the Fulper Potteries in New Jersey, experimented with bisque doll heads as a substitute for the German importations which had been cut off due to the war. After World War I, a few bisque heads came from England, having been produced by disabled war veterans at various English potteries. They were not very good or very numerous.

Bisque heads were used on cloth, kid or composition bodies. Sometimes, bisque hands and feet were made to match the heads, although it was more usual to have the feet of kid or the body material. The shoulder-head style or the swivel neck were both used for bisque heads.

While the German manufacturers produced quantity, the French concentrated on quality and style. Towards the end of the 19th century, however, the German manufacturers were producing bisque heads that were as delicately modeled and detailed as the French ones. The German factories, with their eye on volume business, made many grades of dolls, ranging from poor to excellent. Therefore, it is necessary to recognize not only a maker's name but to also recognize the fine points of modeling, coloring, expression and details of eyes, wigs, etc. To further complicate matters, many French dolls had bisque heads made in Germany which were sent to France for assembling with the French-made bodies. The French kid bodies are by far the finest ever made.

Books and photographs and sketches give only a partial story. It is absolutely necessary to handle, examine and compare as many dolls as you can. Before long you will begin to spot the subtle differences that make one doll better than another. In the meantime, the following names and terms will make you conversant with doll language.

FRENCH BISQUE:

While this particular type of bisque was made in Germany as well as France, it was used to denote the best grade. Its distinguishing feature lies in the fact that a delicate flesh color is ground into the clay before modeling and firing. It has an almost translucent tone that is particularly beautiful. The bisques of the late 19th century are much more highly colored, although they still approximate the natural skin colors somewhat on the rosy side.

SUGAR BISQUE:

This is a low-grade bisque, dead white in tone, having much the same look in texture as day old seven-minute frosting. The cheeks, eyes, mouth, etc., are painted on and, because of the contrast with the dead white, look rather garish.

JUMEAU:

French manufacturer of bisque heads and kid or cloth bodies. Deliberately setting out to make the most beautiful dolls in the world, Jumeau and his son can justly claim that reputation. Stationary, blown glass eyes of great beauty are characteristic of the early dolls. Later ones used the "sleeping eyes." The very earliest Jumeaus, from 1844 to the mid-50's, were good but, as far as the heads were concerned, unequal to those produced from the mid-50's to the 80's. These earlier heads were imported from Germany as was customary with all French doll makers. The very first Jumeaus commanded attention especially for their exquisite gowns and wardrobes. In the early 60's, Jumeau's son took out a patent for attaching a swivel neck to the bust which, at first, was also of bisque. It was about this time that Jumeau engaged in the actual manufacture of bisque heads in France. As the fashion for more childlike dolls grew (the 80's), the bodies were made of composition of papier mâché, only the head being made of bisque. When the composition bodies began to be used, the first identifying marking was introduced, usually on the body, rarely on the head. The success of the Jumeau factory was phenomenal. About the 80's, German interests entered the business, and, in a relatively short time, finally took over the entire company. With the advent of German ownership came a difference in the modeling of the faces which became slightly heavier around the jawline and under the chin.

Bru:

Another French manufacturer of dolls, who, encouraged by the success of the Jumeau factory, engaged in the making of the complete doll's head and body. Bru dolls are usually marked on the lower left side of the back of the bust, with the letters B R U placed vertically. These dolls, while attractive, were seldom as pretty or as fine as the Jumeau heads.

Armand Marseille:

The dolls from this French manufacturer have bisque heads, clearly marked as having been made in Germany and having all of the characteristics of the German style of modeling. They frequently were patented in France. Earlier ones (late 70's, early 80's) were the shoulder-head type with lovely blown glass eyes.

Simon & Halbig:

The bisque heads from this German manufacturer are well modeled, sometimes exceptionally so. This is a comparatively modern firm and its heads are on the large side. The name "Simon & Halbig" is almost always accompanied by another name or initials used with a symbol. That name is Heinrich Handwerck.

The differences between this Simon and Halbig doll and the Jumeau doll are very subtle. Without examining incised trademarks (which both have) it is uncertain at best to definitely attribute dolls of this style to one or the othe rof the manufacturers. This one, 28 inches tall, wears a real child's dress of the 1900 period in which she was made.

An 1890 Jumeau with swivel neck, pierced ears and blonde hair. The composition body and limbs are characteristic of both the Jumeaus and the Simon Halbig (German) dolls of the period. Her clothes are original and she's 22 inches tall.

K & R:

Which is usually separated with a six-pointed star which has the symbol "&" in the center. An interesting conjecture arises. Were special lines of dolls made for Simon & Halbig by K & R and Heinrich Handwerck much as special styles are "made expressly for B. Altman & Co. by Fownes"? At any rate, these dolls date after 1891 when they also carry the legend "Made in Germany."

J. D. KESTNER:

German manufacturer of both "French" bisque heads and fine bodies.

BLOWN GLASS EYE:

A particularly beautiful type of eye having great depth and naturalness. Both iris and pupil are well defined. Used in both shoulder-head and swivel-neck styles, the blown glass eye is always stationary. The use of these eyes was not confined exclusively to the bisque head. They are to be seen in china (rarely), composition, celluloid and Parian.

CLOSED TOP HEAD:

Those doll heads of bisque designed for the addition of a wig had openings of some diameter where the crown of the head normally would be. Several reasons have been advanced for this device: to make the heads lighter or to facilitate the insertion of eyes, or to cut down import taxes. Very rarely, a bisque head would have a closed top with two holes in it for tying on the wig. The closed top was more common in wax, composition and papier mâché.

PIERCED EARS:

Many bisque heads had holes in the lobes of the ears for earrings. This mode, popular in the 1880's for little girls, was duplicated in their dolls. The style persisted, in dolls, through the 90's and slightly beyond.

BALL JOINTS:

With the increasing demand for child-dolls and the growth of composition or papier mâché bodies combined with bisque heads, we see the ball joint appear. About the 1880's, the demand for child-dolls became quite evident. Papier mâché or

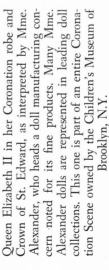

Queen Elizabeth II in her Coronation robe and Crown of St. Edward, as interpreted by Mme. Alexander, who heads a doll manufacturing concern noted for its fine products. Many Mme. Alexander dolls are represented in leading doll collections. This one is part of an entire Coronation Scene owned by the Children's Museum of Brooklyn, N.Y.

This Greiner head on a crudely made body bears comparison with the elegant Greiner on page 166. That one was obviously dressed by a professional or an exceptionally skilled home dressmaker. This one speaks for itself. The styling of the hair and eyes of this one dates her as being somewhat older than the blonde Greiner.

A FINE LENCI DOLL

This is an exquisite example of the famous Lenci doll from Turin, Italy, made in the 1920's. The doll is felt as are the main parts of her costume. She is dressed as a Swiss shepherdess.

composition bodies were substituted for the kid and cloth ones of previous years which had been most frequently designed as "lady" dolls. To give the desired articulation, ball joints of wood were inserted between the upper and lower limbs, less frequently at the wrists. This type of joint, modeled on the lay figure, made it possible for the doll to be put into extremely lifelike poses. The dolls were strung (parts held together) with elastic cord.

PARIAN:

An exceptionally fine form of china so named because of its resemblance to the lovely marble from the Isle of Paros, Greece. Made from a hard, clear paste that lent itself to exquisite detail and delicate modeling. The majority of Parian heads come under the classification of "fancies" due to the elaborate details added to the shoulder-head; i.e., flowers, ribbons, snoods, combs, guimpes, etc. Touches of gold luster were frequently used to highlight these details.

BENNINGTON:

While some collectors and dealers use this name to identify certain doll heads, it has been proven beyond argument that the famous Bennington potteries in Vermont never made doll heads. This is equally true of the manufacturers below.

CHELSEA AND STAFFORDSHIRE:

Famous English potteries who have absolutely no records or have found no fragments to indicate that doll heads had ever been manufactured there.

MEISSEN:

Fine porcelain from the China Manufactory at Meissen, Germany. An indisputable method of identification is by means of the crossed swords printed in cobalt blue, under the glaze, inside the head or inside back of shoulder piece. Many lovely Meissen figurines exist, but few doll heads.

DRESDEN:

Another famous German name signifying delicate heads with elaborate decorative details. Whether these doll heads actually are the product of Dresden manufactories is debatable.

BONNET DOLLS:
Any doll head having a bonnet, cap or other form of hat is called a Bonnet Doll.

WAX

MONTANARI:
Finest maker of English wax dolls. Beautifully modeled and extremely lifelike. The originator, Madame Augusta Montanari, followed by her son Richard, produced wax dolls over a period from 1850 to the late 1880's. Examination of some wax heads shows an incised "M" inside the shoulder. It is believed that this stands for Montanari.

PAPIER MÂCHÉ AND COMPOSITION

GREINER:
First American manufacturers (1840) of doll heads, styled like German china models, hence the similarity in hair-dos and faces. Only reliable way to indisputably identify a Greiner is by its label. The patented details of the Greiner heads, after expiration of their patents, were picked up and duplicated by other manufacturers.

HOLZ-MASSE:
Used together with a trademark design which looks like a cuspidor in which a bird is nesting, from the back of which extends a stick having a knob on top and wings. Considerable argument about meaning of phrase or name. It is also found on wax-over-composition heads, as well as on cloth bodies.

DOTTER AND GOLDSMITH:
These two manufacturers also used composition or papier mâché heads as well as the china heads.

SUPERIOR:
This name is always preceded by either of two sets of initials: M & S Superior or G L Superior. A serial number is also included on the label. While contemporary with the Greiners, the place of origin of the Superior is debatable.

DEWEES COCHRAN:
Modern artist and doll designer whose dolls were made of composition. Modeled to resemble American children, they are slender and graceful.

The array of twentieth century dolls made of composition is tremendous. Shirley Temple, Deanna Durbin, Judy Garland are a few of the screen stars who have served as models for dolls. A legion of story-book characters in doll form, duplicates of radio stars and Margit Nilsen's "Deb-U" and "Little Sister," add to the endless list of composition dolls.

RUBBER AND CELLULOID

GOODYEAR:
First to patent method of making hard rubber. Not a manufacturer of doll's heads.

BRU:
French manufacturer of mid-19th century, patented a rubber baby doll in 1878.

MARGIT NILSEN:
Rubber fashion doll of the 1940's having natural hair.

I. R. COMB CO.:
Or I.R.C., stands for India Rubber Comb Co., manufacturers of rubber dolls for display purposes. About 1860.

MAGIC-SKIN:
Modern rubber baby doll. While head is of plastic, the body and limbs are of hollow rubber that looks and feels, wrinkles and indents, like human skin.

TORTOISE:
Or turtle, a design used as a trademark on fine German-made celluloid dolls.

Since the majority of celluloid dolls were manufactured from the 1880's on, there is little trouble in identifying them as, by that time, the custom of labeling was quite common.

RAG DOLLS

CHASE STOCKINET:

An all-rag doll designed by Mrs. Martha J. Chase of Pawtucket, R. I., in the late 80's. By the middle 90's she started the commercial manufacture of this doll under her own supervision. First a toy, the Chase Stockinet Doll developed into specifically designed dolls for hospitals where they are currently used for training purposes. The toy doll was never patented, but always carried the trade mark of a round baby face surmounted by the legend, "The Chase Stockinet Doll," printed either on the left leg between hip and knee, or just under the left arm.

COLUMBIAN DOLL:

Designed and made by Emma E. Adams of Oswego Center, N. Y. Dolls were so named because they were accepted for exhibit at the Chicago World's Fair in 1893, by the Columbian Commission. The doll received a diploma of merit.

KATHE KRUSE:

Wife of noted German sculptor, she designed particularly appealing child-dolls made of moisture-proof nettle cloth and stuffed with reindeer hair. Faces have the charming seriousness of very young children. First appeared about Christmas, 1910.

BERNARD RAVCA:

Made in France during the 20's, the Ravca rag dolls were actually character studies of French peasants, accurately costumed and having extraordinarily well modeled faces of soft cotton covered with silk stocking material.

LENCI:

Made in Turin, Italy, by Madame Lenci, these dolls appeared in the early 20's. Beautifully modeled, winsome child faces, and chubby arms and legs, all of peach felt, the Lenci dolls were fancifully and elaborately dressed. Main parts of costumes were also made of felt.

20th CENTURY DOLLS BY AMERICAN DESIGNERS

Americans have always been doll makers . . . of one sort or another. Mothers, grandmothers, aunts, even uncles and fathers have turned out homemade dolls. Some were skillfully executed, others were inept, but all had an endearing quality implicit in their birth. They were made to delight children. Even after the manufacturing of dolls became widespread and their prices were within the means of a greater number of people, the homemade doll continued to flourish for a variety of reasons, not the least of which was the delight and satisfaction it gave its maker. The few early ones that have survived hold treasured places in today's museums and private collections and seem not at all abashed by the beautiful, sophisticated commercial beauties in whose company they find themselves.

The handmade doll of the 20th century is a far cry from those early ones. She too may be of cloth (the rag doll but with a difference), as are those made by Dorothy Heizer, Madame Perrault, Gwen Flather: carved wood has a number of devotees including Helen Bullard, creator of the Holly Dolls, and Ruth Williams, known as "Darcy," whose wooden dolls were jointed in much the manner of Penny Woodens.

A goodly number of 20th century American doll designers prefer to work in ceramics, bisque or porcelain while other individualists create with plastic wood, various compositions and poured wax. Constant experiment with various materials devised by themselves or from commercial sources has made possible the stamping of high individuality by each artist on her creations . . . an individuality that is immediately recognizable by knowing collectors.

It is fortunate that so many contemporary doll artists have learned that the sewn-on label is the least reliable means of identification. Like string tags, they are so easily lost or removed. Muriel Bruyere always puts her name or initials on the foot of her doll before it is fired, and Martha Thompson uses the initials MDT on the shoulder together with the date. Magge Head's name and the date of production are incised on the shoulders of

This 13-inch German celluloid-headed doll was made in 1928. Her body, arms and legs are of cloth and her peasant style clothes are of no particular region. What distinguishes her is the trademark impressed on the back of the celluloid shoulder—a turtle within a lozenge, which signifies that she was made by the Rheinische Gummi und Celluloid Fabrik Co.

her dolls. Helen Bullard's carved wooden dolls are signed and dated on the body. Fawn Zeller's early dolls bore labels but the later ones have her name or initials on the back of the doll. Both Dewees Cochran and Avis Lee, whose dolls have been commercially reproduced in substantial quantities, have distinctive tags that identify them. Gwen Flather's dolls, with their finely needle-modeled faces, are tagged "Strawberry Patch Doll."

The above artists, together with a good many more of equal ability and originality, provide the new doll collector with an intriguing and varied field to study, to search out. Their dolls are choice acquisitions which will increase in value as the years go on and will always be stars in your collection.

Index

INDEX